BLAH, BLAH, BLAH

Don't Tell Me—
Show Me!

Keeping your words and actions
consistent, congruent and
grounded in integrity

International
Best-selling author

Tim Connor

BLAH, BLAH, BLAH: Don't Tell Me—Show Me!

Editor: Catherine Frenzel

ISBN: 1-930376-19-7

Published by: Worldwide Press

First Printing: May 2013

For information on Tim's services as a meeting or convention speaker, please:

Call: 704-895-1230

Write: Connor Resource Group, Box 397, Davidson, NC 28036

Email: tim@timconnor.com

Websites:

www.timconnor.com

www.OvercomingLifeChallenges.com

www.Blahs.biz

"What you are speaks so loudly that I cannot hear what you say."

~ Ralph Waldo Emerson

A few of Tim's best-selling books

Fail Often So You Can Succeed Sooner

Your First Year in Sales

The Trade-Off

The Ancient Scrolls

Where Did All Those Years Go?

O.K. God, What's Next?

From Loneliness to Solitude

Peace of Mind

The Last Goodbye

The Male Gift-Giving Survival Guide

Life is Short

Above Ground

Success Is a Decision

That's Life!

Soft Sell

The Road to Happiness is Full of Potholes

Corporate Disconnect

81 Challenges Smart Managers Face

Dedication

To Marlene –

I have searched for my entire life to find someone who always had the courage and the ability to be honest with their words and have integrity between their words and their actions. One day she miraculously came into my life, and my life would never be the same.

Contents

Introduction

Words are easy and, often, as the expression goes, 'cheap'.

Why do so many people say things they don't mean, or have no intention of honoring them when they are saying them?

Or why do people say things when they don't even know what they really mean? *Blah, blah, blah.*

You've heard it, we've all heard it: *Don't tell me—show me.*

In the following pages, I'll discuss the why's, when's, how's and what-if's involving the use of words and their impact on relationships, success and just plain happiness and inner peace.

It's becoming easier and easier for people today to just say things like:

- I need my space.
- I love you.
- I want you.
- I need you.
- I feel let down.
- You disappointed me.
- You promised.
- You said . . .
- I promise . . .
- I will . . .

Why are words so important when it comes to our personal integrity and the impact of words on others in our lives?

Why do people knowingly or even unknowingly say things they don't mean, understand or intend?

Why do we let others set us up with their words, promises and commitments?

Why do words often create so much disappointment, frustration, resentment, and even anger or fear?

These questions could go on and on, but the core question is: Why is there often a disconnect between words and actions?

The main purpose of this book is two-fold:

1. to help you understand the impact your words have on others and even yourself, and
2. to grasp how others' words affect us and our relationships with them.

Is disappointment a reality? Of course.

Can we always control the outcomes connected with our words? Of course not.

Do situations arise that we couldn't anticipate, that will change an outcome in a heartbeat? Yes.

The question is: Is the relationship grounded in respect, understanding, acceptance and the awareness that *life happens?*

Life happens. I know it does. I have had numerous situations in my career, relationships and life in general where I wanted something to happen, believed it would, shared this with others and then—BAM—it didn't.

Welcome to the real world.

However, this doesn't mean that you shouldn't do your very best at all times to communicate with clarity, honesty and an understanding that life can't be controlled one hundred percent of the time.

One final thought as you make your way through the following pages: Words can be paradoxical and they can be emotional triggers.

For example, "You are always so thoughtful." Or, "You are always so critical." How about, "You never thank me." Or, "You never embarrass me in public."

How about a few emotional triggers:

- You should . . .
- You don't . . .
- You better . . .

- You must . . .
- You need to . . .

Notice the common denominator in all of them: YOU. Effective communication is a two-way street: the accuracy of how a message is sent and how it is interpreted. Both contribute to the outcome of any correlation between words and actions.

So, friends, let's get started. Have fun learning how to create better congruence between what you say and what you do.

~ Tim Connor

Words, just words

Because I am an author and speaker, words are my stock-in-trade. Their meaning, intent and all the ways that a simple word can be interpreted can create varying degrees of responses.

For example, when you say things like the following to someone, what can these words or phrases mean?

- right away
- soon
- never
- always
- It depends.
- I'll consider it.
- I meant ...
- You said ...
- I love you.
- You never ...
- I need my space.
- I promise.
- etc.

Every word or phrase we all use can be interpreted in many different ways by everyone. In fact, if we said to ten different people, *I'll get to it as soon as I can*, do you think this simple phrase would set up different expectations in each of these ten people?

The answer is, *yes!* But why?

There are numerous reasons. Here are just a few of the most common ones:

1. We all have unique mental perceptual filters.
2. We all have unique emotional perceptual filters.
3. We all have different expectations.
4. We all have varying degrees of experience.
5. We all have different agendas.
6. We all have unique fears.

7. We all interpret messages and words uniquely.
8. We all have unique ways of communicating.
9. We all have different upbringing and conditioning.
10. We all have different levels of education.
11. We all have unique desires, dreams and needs.
12. We all have egos.

Get it? We are all different in so many ways. So, when you use a simple phrase like, *I'll get to this as soon as I can*--it's to be expected that everyone may hear a totally different message than was intended or even sent.

The key to improving understanding and reducing conflict in communication —regardless of whether it is with a customer, your spouse, a friend or an employee—is to have a simple system of ensuring clarity and reducing misunderstanding caused by any of the reasons indicated above.

Try an experiment right now. Open your dictionary (if you still have one; or your online dictionary) and look up the word *negative*. What did you find? Well, I'll help you out here:

- Damaging
- Depressing
- Harmful
- Downbeat
- Unhelpful
- Unconstructive
- Refusal
- Denial
- Disapproving
- Unenthusiastic
- Bad
- Less than zero
- Opposite of positive
- Uncooperative
- Pessimistic
- Blaming
- Opposing
- Undesirable

And this is just half of the definitions presented.

So, when someone says, *You are being negative,* what do they mean? Well, pick any of the above variations and you might be right. However, if when they said it, they meant that you were being *unhelpful*—and you interpreted *negative* as *disapproving*—do you think maybe an argument might follow?

The average person has a vocabulary of about 1500 words. How many words do you think there are in the modern dictionary? Well, if you guessed 25,000-50,000, you're not even close. Read the following:

> *There is no single sensible answer to this question. It's impossible to count the number of words in a language, because it's so hard to decide what actually counts as a word. Is* dog *one word or two (a noun meaning 'a kind of animal', and a verb meaning 'to follow persistently')? If we count it as two, then do we count inflections separately, too (e.g.,* dogs *= plural noun,* dogs *= present tense of the verb)? Is* dog-tired *a word, or just two other words joined together? Is* hot dog *really two words, since it might also be written as* hot-dog *or even* hotdog?
>
> *It's also difficult to decide what counts as 'English'. What about medical and scientific terms? Latin words used in law, French words used in cooking, German words used in academic writing, Japanese words used in martial arts? Do you count Scots dialect? Teenage slang? Abbreviations?*
>
> *The Second Edition of the 20-volume Oxford English Dictionary [OED] contains full entries for 171,476 words in current use, and 47,156 obsolete words. To this may be added around 9,500 derivative words included as subentries. Over half of these words are nouns, about a quarter adjectives, and about a seventh verbs; the rest is made up of exclamations, conjunctions, prepositions, suffixes, etc. And these figures don't take account of entries with senses for different word classes (such as noun and adjective).*
>
> *This suggests that there are, at the very least, a quarter of a million distinct English words, excluding inflections, and words from technical and regional vocabulary not covered by the OED, or words not yet added to the published dictionary, of which perhaps 20 percent are no longer in current use. If distinct tenses were*

> *counted, the total would probably approach three quarters of a million.*

(Sorry, I've had this quote for so long that I don't remember the source.)

So, is it possible that when you use a word, you or the other person either:

- don't know what it means?
- are not aware of all of the possible meanings?
- use it incorrectly?
- send the wrong message?
- insult someone?
- invalidate someone?
- humiliate someone?
- confuse someone?

The answer to all of these questions could be – or more accurately, is—a resounding, YES.

How do we avoid all of these word or communication errors? Learn the meaning of all 250,000-plus words in the English language? Make sure the people we are communicating with do the same?

Impossible—both 'solutions'. So, what's the answer? That's what this book is about: creating congruence between words and actions. The problem is: If you don't know the meaning of a word or how it is being understood or even heard by someone else, or if they have a similar situation going on in their brain—well, you're headed for conflict, confusion, misunderstanding and an often less-than-desirable outcome.

The solution to this problem is the ability to be congruent: to be similar, the same or to agree. In this book, when I use the word *congruent*, I am applying the definition *to be the same*. In other words, if you say, "I'll do it", you do it, no matter what. However, be careful when you say you'll do something such as:

- be on time,
- return a phone call,
- accomplish something.

There may be extenuating circumstances that you can't control that may contradict the outcome that you said would happen. Ever been there? I have.

So, as you read through the examples, stories, illustrations and ideas that follow, keep one question in mind:

As I say in the subtitle, *Don't Tell Me—Show Me,* ***how can you ensure that there is always congruence between your words and your actions?***

Some basics

Self-disclosure

One of the best books I have ever read on the subject of self-disclosure is *The Transparent Self* by Sidney M. Jourard. In it he explains in simple terms the importance of understanding and integrating this valuable skill into all of our communication.

What exactly is self-disclosure?

We all have varying degrees of self-knowledge and understanding. We also have our little secrets about who we are, what we believe, what we feel and when—as well as opinions and values and the varying degrees of comfort of sharing them with friends, strangers or family members.

Self-disclosure is when you are willing to let others into your personal zone of attitudes, beliefs and values that express who you really are and what you really feel or believe.

Simply put, self-disclosure is communicating often-private information about yourself to others.

The thing to remember is that too little or too much self-disclosure builds barriers in relationships, while balanced self-disclosure builds bridges.

Let's say that I were to share with you all of my fears, frustrations, failures, problems, concerns and shortcomings. I can hear you now: "I don't need that much information about you to get value from this book. I don't enjoy pitying others, especially when I paid twenty bucks for this book."

Or the opposite: What if I shared with you all of my successes, achievements, highs, accomplishments, etc.? I can also hear you now, "You arrogant SOB, who do you think you are, better than me?!"

You see, in both of these cases, too much self-disclosure did not contribute to a mutually beneficial relationship between us.

Balanced self-disclosure is when I share enough (the appropriate amount about myself, given the nature of our relationship) to create a connection where we have some common ground.

For example, let's say I told you that I have had my share of communication breakdowns with others or that I have said things I didn't mean. This simple disclosure sends the message that I am no different than you, as we all do this from time to time. If I had said I have never done this, well, you might just become a bit suspicious of me and my motives, thinking, "Man, have you got an out-of-control ego, thinking you are perfect in this area!"

Well, I'm not perfect at all. I struggle every day with creating consistency between my words and actions. There, I've said it: I'm normal. I'm just like everyone else and I, too, struggle with communication breakdowns.

My point is that I have tried to create common ground between us, a connection where we are both normal and similar when it comes to this issue. With this simple self-disclosure, I have prepared the way for a sort of bond between us where you will tend to be more willing to learn from my mistakes and counsel. But, what if I had gone on for a few pages, sharing story after story where I have screwed up in this area. Again, I can hear you say, "How do you feel you have the right to write a book about this stuff when you haven't even figured it out yourself?"

Bottom line: Self-disclosure takes courage, understanding, compassion and a willingness to be real and vulnerable.

Detachment vs. disengagement

There is a dramatic difference between detachment and disengagement. Detachment is when I am not responsible for you:

- I am not responsible for your feelings.
- I am not responsible for your outcomes.
- I am not responsible for your attitudes.
- I am not responsible for the consequences of your actions.
- I am not responsible for the consequences of your decisions.
- I am not responsible for your behaviors.
- I am not responsible for your stress.

When I detach from your stuff, and it is your stuff, I let you grow and learn what life wants you to learn from your errors in judgment, mistakes and actions. I am there to support you and help you where you feel I can help—

but you must do the work.

Disengagement is where, not only do I detach, but I don't even care what is happening to you or why, when or how. I have completely cut you off emotionally. I just don't give a rip.

Detachment helps others grow, learn and develop if you will let them. Disengagement puts distance, often irreparable distance, between you and another person.

Invalidators

What is an invalidator? It is a person who puts other people down, insults them in public, disregards their opinions, does not listen, lets their own ego try to control the other person, is emotionally manipulative, or negates the other person's feelings. Not a pretty picture is it? Invalidators are everywhere: in homes, the classrooms, the boardroom, on the golf course and in the bedroom. I have had the fortune (and misfortune) to have had several invalidators in my life.

It isn't fun. They give you the opportunity to hide under a rock, lock yourself in the closet, fight back or give up and run. I have done all of the above. How do you know if you work with (or for), live with or just hang out with an invalidator? Here are a few clues:

1. They interrupt you a lot.
2. They ignore or don't really care about your feelings.
3. They say things like: *you should, you never, you always, you don't, you owe me.*
4. They say *don't you…?* rather than *do you…?*
5. They don't listen to you.
6. They are so wrapped up in themselves that you don't really exist.
7. They are concerned only about their own needs and don't give a rip about yours.
8. They communicate things like: *What will people think?* Or, *You make me angry.*
9. They also can be heard saying: *How could you do that to me? See what you made me do? It is your fault. If you really loved me you would…. Why can't you be more like….? I expect you to….*

There is a lot more, but I am sure you can now identify if you are an invalidator or if you have one in your life.

Here is one thing you *can't* do: Change them.

But there are a few things you can do if you have one in your life:

1. Accept their behavior. (It most likely will never change.)
2. Leave.
3. Get yourself, them or both of you into therapy.
4. Record your conversations and play them back.
5. Read the book *Nasty People* by Jay Carter.
6. Have a signal you can use every time the other person invalidates you. For example, whenever they interrupt, you can tap their hand (I just made that up).
7. Ask a third party to act as an observer. Whenever the other person invalidates you, the observer can tell the other person.
8. Develop some rules of behavior in the relationship.
9. You can respond to their statements with things like: *I am sorry you feel I should have acted differently. It might not be acceptable to you, but I have chosen to do it.*

The key here is to not take personal ownership of the other person's opinions, values, criticisms or judgments.

Words that heal

When we string together different words in our communication, we can trigger anger, frustration, happiness, sadness, and limitless other emotions in the other person. There are, however, a few very short sentences that can go a long way towards healing a relationship that might be stressful, frustrating or difficult. Some of these are:

- I understand.
- Please forgive me.
- I am sorry.
- I like you just the way you are.
- I forgive you.
- You are right.
- It's going to be okay.
- I accept you.

The opposite of these affirmations can contribute to continued on-going strife. They are:

- You are wrong.
- You need to change.
- Don't do [whatever].
- I can never forgive you.
- You don't understand.
- You should... can't... never... won't....

How about spending the next few days listening to your own words and reactions to what other people do, say and feel as a result of them. Are your reactions and words filled with:

- acceptance or challenge,
- validation or denial,
- resistance or endorsement,
- love or anger,
- blame or tolerance,
- resentment or humility?

In my years of relationships, I have been on the receiving end of both positive and negative reinforcements from others, and I can tell you, unequivocally, that when their words are sent with understanding, acceptance and love, they go a long way in healing—not only you, but themselves as well. But when the words and ideas you choose to send are filled with negative overtones or intent, they will contribute to continued stress and negative outcomes for both of you.

Let's summarize. What I am talking about here is being nice, kind and loving with someone vs. intolerant, hateful and non-accepting. I suggest you take a close look at some of your relationships that seem to be filled with anxiety and stress, to see how your words may be contributing to less-than-favorable conditions—regardless of whether you are on the giving or receiving end.

Personal blind spots

Blind spots are those areas in your own behavior that when someone points them out to you, you just don't see it, or say "That's not me" or "You have to be kidding"—whatever. Blind spots are when someone says that you have certain habits, beliefs or behaviors that he or she believes could be destructive for the future health of your relationship or for yourself, but you fail to accept this as a part of who you are or how you behave. If someone is not saying these things in a negative way or criticizing or invalidating you, but is merely reporting information to you, giving you the opportunity to see the need or benefits for change, it is important to be willing to listen without judgment or defensiveness.

Eliminating many of these blind spots can help you get better in touch with the reality of your own behaviors and their impact on your relationships and the overall quality of your life.

There are many types of denial and there are a variety of reasons that may cause this denial. A few of them are:

1. The blind spots I just mentioned
2. In some way, you are contributing to the stress in your relationship.
3. You have hidden agendas or topics that you are uncomfortable discussing, for whatever reason.
4. You are unwilling to take full responsibility for your own actions and/or their outcomes.
5. You are defensive when your partner brings up topics that you disagree with.
6. You are angry when someone mentions your apparent need for growth in some area.
7. You withdraw from discussions that cause you discomfort.
8. You are unable to handle conflict or confrontation in a constructive way.
9. You believe that your opinions are the only ones that are right or valuable.

I could go on, but I am confident that I either have your attention by now, or I don't. If I don't: Before you toss this subject out as just the ranting of a senile old lunatic, ask yourself: Could you be in denial that you are even incapable of having any challenges with any of the above issues?

One way to get to the core of this issue, if you have the courage, is to ask someone you trust a few simple questions. Before you do, though, I suggest you set up a few ground rules: No invalidation, criticism or judgments are allowed. Just a neutral sharing of information. It is also important that both of you ensure that your mental perceptual filters are clear of any obstructions or old emotional baggage. Then ask:

1. What do you think I might be in denial about?
2. How do I behave or talk when you perceive that I am in denial?
3. How do you feel about me when I am in denial?
4. What does my denial do to our relationship?

Just a few thoughts to get you started; how about seeing if you can come up with a few more. The purpose is for personal awareness and enlightenment. Once you have finished this discussion, now reverse roles and you ask the other person the same questions.

Better self-knowledge

Few people know everything about themselves. Over the years, we have developed personal stories that are nothing more than our interpretation of life's events and circumstances. Many of these stories are not at all grounded in truth or reality, but have—over time—etched their way into our minds as real. Self-knowledge helps us realize which of the stories we tell are real versus those that are nothing more than fabrications or how we have interpreted life's events. When we share one of our stories with others, we instinctively know whether it is true or just a made-up version. This give us the opportunity to deal only in truth and shed many of these fabrications, or even lies, we have told ourselves and others over the years.

More intimacy in your relationships

Intimacy is not just between people of the opposite sex, but an emotional connection that is created in a relationship that is based in trust, openness, respect and common ground. When we are more prone to be open to others, we tend to create more intimate relationships with them.

As a speaker, regardless of the size of my audience, one of my major objectives is to create a professionally-appropriate intimate relationship with both the audience in general and with everyone individually in some way.

I attempt to accomplish this by sharing real examples (self-disclosure) from my life that illustrate and reinforce the topic I am discussing.

Over the years, I have discovered that when I am successful in this attempt, the audience always receives more value from my message.

People tend to have a greater degree of trust when the people in their lives are more open and honest.

Improved communication

Needless to say, back-and-forth communication improves dramatically when self-disclosure and self-knowledge are a part of the give-and-take between all parties in a conversation. As you will see in the following sections, those who self-disclose tend to have more integrity in their message and its delivery.

Improved trust

Ever listened to a politician give a speech or an interview with the media? If you have, I'll guarantee that more often than not, what you heard was what they thought you wanted to hear, rather than what they really felt or believed. Is it any wonder, then, why most people don't trust politicians?

Trust is the fundamental ingredient in all successful relationships. The more you know about someone and still like them, the more you will tend to trust them. This isn't always the case; but in general, trust must be the foundation if a relationship is to stand the test of time.

Trust leaves a relationship when someone betrays us in some way, either physically or emotionally. We feel let down or disappointed in some way. I'll talk more about trust later in the book; but for now, know that the greater the trust, the more open and honest the communication.

Less personal guilt

Guilt is nothing more than personal feelings of shame or regret for an act, word or deed done or not done. From a communication perspective, guilt tends to close people off. If I feel guilty about something I did or said, or didn't do or didn't say, I will tend to edit my communication or even totally withdraw from you. I feel ashamed, and the more I am asked to confront this issue, the more guilt I feel. So, to avoid these negative feelings, I will go out of my way to have the least communication with you or avoid contact altogether.

Think about the last time someone phoned you, and you listened to their voice message as they delivered it; you didn't answer the phone because for whatever reason, you didn't want to talk with them at that time. Yes, there might have been various reasons; but I'll bet on some occasions, you just didn't want to have to deal with—whatever—from them right then.

Better connections with others

Think for a moment of people you like to be around. Now ask yourself: What is it about these people that makes you want to spend more time with them? I'll bet it's because you know more about them; but also, when you are with them, you always learn something new or feel better about yourself.

Now think for a moment about someone you know that you don't know a lot about, and when you are with them they are not open or don't share feelings, fears, hopes, dreams, desires—whatever—with you. Each time you are with them, there is no new learning about who they are or what they feel, value or believe; therefore, the connection with them gets weaker and weaker as time passes.

I'll also bet that if you look at the people who have come and gone in your life for whatever reason—whether a personal or romantic relationship or a business one or even a friend—that, with time, you didn't ever get to the point where there was vulnerable sharing and openness.

More compassion for others

The more you know about someone else, the more you will tend to have understanding and compassion for what they are going through or have gone through in the past. Your respect for them will increase over time due to their willingness to trust you with their vulnerability. As a result, a relationship with this person will tend to strengthen over time and be based on mutual respect and trust.

Less stress in your life

Stress is caused not by what is happening in our life, but by how we have learned to respond to these stressors. When a person is under stress, they will tend to shut down in their communication patterns. One of the ways to relieve the impact of this stress is to have people in your life with whom you can honestly share your fears, concerns and frustrations; and you know their response will have no criticism, judgment or retribution.

We call this the ability to 'cathart' or to share, unload or just talk about what concerns you have or are afraid of. When you have someone in your life to fill this role, your trust in them will increase and you will feel a certain intimate connection with them.

This isn't about advice, counsel, suggestions or answers for your challenges; it's about someone who will listen who cares.

Expressing

Everyone expresses themselves in unique ways. While some people are very direct in their responses or messages, others will tend to be less assertive. Neither approach is right or wrong. The critical fact is simply: Is your message; clear, appropriate, understandable, timely and engaging?

Let's take a brief look at each of these characteristics.

Is your message clear?

As you will read in the following sections, every message has the potential for confusion, due to any number of factors. Clarity in communication is one of the major challenges to congruence. If your message can be misunderstood, it most likely already has been. Clarity requires many ingredients from both parties, such as active listening, vocabulary that both understand and a willingness to be engaged in the dialog.

Is your message appropriate?

Appropriate: to be suitable for the occasion or circumstances. By *being appropriate*, I mean that your message is relevant to the other person or the situation. For example: I am trying to get my five year old to understand the concept of responsibility, so I tell him about how I was taught this vital personal behavior by my father. He may have difficulty relating to my illustration since he doesn't have the same degree of life experience or is living in an entirely different time, which has little relevance to when I was his age. But if I choose an analogy based in *his* world or experience, it is more likely to be appropriate.

Is your message understandable?

It takes more than the right words to have your message understood. If the other person can't relate to your rationale or the experience that is contributing to your message, they might not 'get it'. For example: I am trying to interest you in changing a behavior by explaining how the new behavior will help you in the future. The problem is that you have a different mental filter that interprets my explanation from your own mindset, and this might not coincide with mine, thereby creating confusion—not to mention resistance.

Is your message timely?

Ever sent an email to someone, expecting a quick response, but hours or even days passed before you got an answer or reaction? Ever sent an email to someone, asking a question, and receive a response... but they failed to even acknowledge or answer your question?

If you are not clear on your expectation for a response, I'll guarantee you will be disappointed with the other person's reaction or reaction time.

Is your message engaging?

Words are words. If you want to create an engaging dialog, it is vital to use stories, examples or illustrations that build on or reinforce your words. For example: I am trying to help you grasp the simple concept that accurate expression is a vital part of effective communication. So, how do I reinforce this simple fact?

Have you ever had someone say to you, "I don't understand?" And your response was, "Why not? I'm being perfectly clear here; what's the problem?"

Here are a few tips for creating optimum expression:

1. Don't ask questions when you are trying to make a statement.
2. Keep the message as indicated above: clear, timely, engaging, appropriate and understandable.
3. Avoid double messages; deal with one topic at a time.
4. Distinguish between observations, feelings and thoughts.
5. Avoid sarcasm if the other person may misinterpret it.
6. Stay in the present; dragging up the past will most likely clutter the message.
7. Keep your judgments and opinions out of the message unless this is the heart of it.
8. Avoid threats or subtle challenges unless this is your intent.

Gender issues

Research has told us for years that men and women communicate and process information differently. To some degree, this is true; but in the larger picture of communication, there are more similarities than differences. Let's take a quick look at some of the differences. It would be impossible in this section to give you all of the research that has contributed to much of the following, but there are many great books on the market today that validate these differences. John Medina's *Brain Rules* and Michael Gurian's *What Could He Be Thinking*? are two of my favorites.

Here are just a few of the differences in brain physiology and function between males and females that will contribute to their use of words, actions and often the confusion, misunderanding or assumptions that can follow. Please note that I'm not implying that behavior by either women or men is better, superior, or related to only one gender or the other. I'm pretty much just giving you the outcome of years of the above-mentioned research.

With men, it's action first and talk later. With women, it's often the opposite.

- Men are less inclined to stop, be patient, listen or communicate emotions verbally.
- Women's brains tend not to take breaks (chill out from stress). They take fewer mental naps.
- Men spend less time than women thinking out their feelings.
- Men tend to put their pursuit of self-worth and personal power first and intimacy second.
- Men tend to relate to others with greater degrees of personal independence than women.
- Men tend to show off their wounds more than women.
- Men want to demonstrate bravery and courage more than women.
- Men tend to seek a calling.
- Men tend to take risks that lead them to step out of moral boundaries more often than women.
- Men tend to live their lives as if they are on a quest of some kind.
- Men tend to delay emotional reactions more than women.

- Men, more than women, will not know what they feel at the moment of feeling and will take longer to figure it out.
- Women are better than men at verbalizing their feelings.
- Men tend to withdraw or put on masks when it comes to expressing feelings.
- Women tend to express feelings, while men tend to release them.
- To men, emotions are to be solved rather than enjoyed.
- Men tend to be more fragile and need more reassurance from others.
- Women tend to be better active-listeners than men.
- Men need to be needed by women more than women need to be needed by men.
- Women want more love, and men want more sex to feel validated.
- Men need women to trust what they do.
- Men are more afraid to become responsible for a woman's happiness than vice versa.
- Men's brain development matures slower than women's, which can create a great deal of confusion as to the differences in behavior, communication and intention.

Let me summarize the above with two easy-to-interpret lists. Keep in mind these are generalizations and by no means applicable for all men or women.

Girls and women:

- seek connection
- prefer interdependence and cooperation
- decide by consensus
- yearn for intimacy
- want approval of their peers
- speak up more in private
- share problems
- focus on details of feelings
- mix business and personal talk

Boys and men:

- seek status
- prefer independence and autonomy
- decide by force, persuasion or majority rule
- yearn for space
- want the respect of their peers
- speak up more in public
- keep promises to themselves
- focus on details of fact
- stick to business

- ask for help, guidance and sympathy
- listen and share
- want to understand problems

- don't ask for help, guidance or advice
- give advice and analysis
- want to solve problems

I could go on and on with these differences as well as similarities, but my point here is simply that because of many of the above communication challenges between men and women—regardless of whether it's in a romantic relationship or some other one—there will always be instances of breakdowns between words, their meaning, their interpretation and the ultimate behaviors and actions.

Hidden agendas

A hidden agenda is simply a communication of some type that is held back, for any number of reasons. The two primary ones are the desire to avoid a conflict or to intentionally hurt the other person emotionally. Hidden agendas will tend to be more prevalent in relationships that are not emotionally safe; in other words, ones that have more criticism, judgments or negative consequences when real thoughts, fears, desires or emotions are shared.

Following are some of the more common reasons for these hidden agendas:

- I'm good, but you're not.
- I'm better than you.
- You're better than me.
- You're good, but I'm not.
- I'm smart, but you aren't.
- I'm smarter than you.
- You're smarter than me.
- I'm helpless.
- I'm blameless.
- I'm fragile.
- I'm tough.
- I know it all.
- You're stronger than me (emotionally).
- I'm stronger than you (emotionally).

Any or all of these inner feelings or attitudes may contribute to a person holding back with a hidden agenda.

Personality differences

There are hundreds of personality assessment tools available today that clearly show there are unique approaches to every conceivable situation, whether business, relationship, travel, goals, fears, etc. We all have a dominant personality type. We all also have a variety of secondary personalities (not talking here about schizophrenia).

Entire books have been written on this subject; for example, William Marston's *Emotions of Normal People* and Kiersey and Bates' *Please Understand Me*. If you want to understand this subject better, I encourage you to read one of them.

The basic premise here is that we are all different in some way, and these differences can have a significant impact on the integrity, interpretation and understanding of any communicated message.

Cultural issues

Having travelled the word as a speaker, I can tell you that culture plays a major role in communication congruence. There are too many countries and too many cultural nuances to adequately discuss them in this section. If you want to better understand a particular culture's uniqueness when it comes to communication, you need to do the research. Just know that they exist and can sabotage communication congruence in a heartbeat.

Technology and communication

Email and texting will never replace personal contact. I know you might think I'm operating in the Dark Ages, but I have heard horror stories about people who believe technology is the latest and greatest way to communicate with others. Why, then, is this a problem for me?

For starters, have you ever sent an email that was misunderstood? Have you ever sent a text to someone who made an erroneous assumption from it? Have you ever sent the same email to ten people and gotten ten different interpretations?

Yes, using technology to keep in touch with the basics is fine, for areas like:

- Knowing that your kids are okay

- Confirming a meeting
- Checking with a spouse while at the grocery store
- Getting directions
- Telling someone you miss them.

Blah, blah, blah.

Here's the problem: Communication is more than words, and technology can transmit *only* words from person to person. I'm not saying that technology is not a good tool to use for the basics, but when you send a potentially emotionally-charged email or text—well, I guarantee that sooner or later, you are going to need a face-to-face or at least a phone conversation with the recipient.

Why are people using these forms of communication more and more?

- It's easier.
- It's faster.
- It's more convenient.
- It's 24/7.
- It keeps things simple (supposedly).
- It keeps people at a distance.

What's the problem with these answers? None, if that's all you want your human interaction to be. But I'm here to tell you that relationships grounded only in such technology will lack a great deal of intimacy, trust and emotional connection.

Intention—communication and action

The foundation of this book is simple: There are words and then there are actions, and both of these are grounded in intention or the lack of it.

There has been a lot written in the past few years about 'intention'. Exactly what is intention?

Without going into a great deal of 'heady' stuff here, intention is one of two things: stated intention and real intention.

Many people say they mean things when they really don't. The contradiction here is an inconsistency between what they say and what they really mean.

We've all been in relationships where people said things, said they meant them and even tried to convince us that their words and intentions were honest and real. But we've all been blind-sided by the lack of integrity behind these so-called intentions.

Without going into the gory details, I can tell you that I've dated a few women who said one thing and meant or did another. Now, I'm not being critical of the female gender here, as men are just as guilty of doing this. This isn't a gender issue, but one of intention.

I've been told, "Our relationship is important to me," "You are important to me,"—blah, blah,blah—but when it came to their actual behavior, it was like night and day, because their words and actions were miles apart.

Yes, there are always unforeseen circumstances that affect what we say and what we then do. But we need to pay attention to trends and subtle signals.

I'm an observant person, more than most people, and maybe this has caused me some of the pain I have experienced in relationships, giving too much credence to people's words. But as humans, what else do we have?

If you say you are going to be on time—and there is a traffic jam, life happens. But if you say you are going to be on time and are always late—well, that's a trend.

I usually have no problem with you being late; however, just stop telling me that you are going to be on time when you know the chances of this, most of the time, are unlikely. Am I being, as many people have told me over the years, "just too sensitive?"

Words are more than words. They are the way we communicate feelings, attitudes, beliefs, fears, hopes, dreams and so on. So, if you keep telling the world you are going to do whatever it takes to accomplish something, and the first time you hit a snag, you give in or up—well, what were your real intentions? What gives words their integrity when it comes to interpretation is two-fold: your intent, and the ability or willingness of the other person to grasp what your meaning is.

It's simple: If you say one thing (stated intention)—I'm going to lose weight—and you don't, well, what do you think your real intention was? You thought you knew, but did you really? So, what's the problem here? Nothing, unless your stated intentions impact me. Or something, if you need to look deeper into the reasons for the disconnect.

Animals don't get disappointed, and why? It's simple: They don't talk. Yes, they communicate, but they don't use words; they use behavior and non-verbal methods of communication. Yes, there are a few exceptions; for example, those African Grey Parrots that talk. I've actually had a conversation with one of them, but I have to wonder, *was this just mimicking or was it thoughtful expression?*

Can dogs smile? No, but can they send you messages that they are happy? Yes. Do cat's laugh? No, but they can send the message that they are in a playful state of mind.

Humans are the only known species that communicates with reasoning or thought on two levels, verbal and non-verbal.

And here's where the trouble begins: when there is inconsistency between the verbal or spoken message and the non-verbal message or signal.

Ever had a person tell you with words that they loved you, but their actions were totally inconsistent with these words? If you haven't, you are fortunate, indeed, and I wish more of us could say the same.

Common communication breakdowns

Everyone has agendas that can often get in the way of their communication with others. These agendas can be positive, but are usually self-serving in some way.

Communication between two people is a challenge at best, for any number of reasons. Here are just a few:

1. Education
2. Vocabulary
3. Emotions or feelings
4. Old emotional baggage
5. Unique ways of expression
6. Different listening skills and ability
7. Ego needs
8. Different conditioned backgrounds
9. Experience
10. Stress
11. Expectations

If these are not enough to routinely sabotage messages that are shared between two people, we could always add:

12. Technology
13. Career and family demands
14. Personal needs and desires
15. Personal rules for how others should feel, act or behave

As you can imagine, for communication to work at all in a positive way, there are many factors that must be considered. Just blurting out words is never enough if you want to create clarity, understanding, acceptance and congruence.

For example, here are just a few of the many things people say that can create misunderstanding, anxiety, frustration or confusion:

1. You don't understand . . .

2. Why did you say that, that way?
3. You know what I mean . . .
4. When I can get to it . . .
5. Let me be perfectly honest with you . . .
6. You said . . .
7. I meant . . .
8. In a little while . . .
9. Some day . . .
10. I'll try . . .

All communication is determined not just by the words used, but by how people interpret them. Ever sent a simple text message to someone and their response, "What did you mean by that?" Or, "Why did you say that, that way?"

Ever sent an email to someone, and they interpreted it completely the opposite of your intended message?

These examples happen millions of times a day in relationships between spouses, parents and children; customers, supervisors and employees, friends and even total strangers.

Part of the problem is that with every communication, whether with someone we've known awhile or have just met, there are numerous factors that each person brings to the interaction. Things like:

1. The history of the relationship
2. Feelings towards the other person
3. Unresolved previous issues or concerns with people
4. The length of the relationship
5. The level of trust and respect in the relationship
6. Hidden agendas
7. How emotionally safe the relationship is
8. Personality-style differences
9. Tension levels in the relationship

If you haven't figured it out by now, if communication is to work, it takes a lot of effort, patience, knowledge, congruent intent, understanding, empathy and often compassion.

Now add to this mix the complicated issue of actual behavior that follows or precedes any dialog, and it's a miracle that communication ever works at all.

So, what are communication breakdowns and how do they impact the quality of a relationship when it comes to words vs. actions or behavior?

Relationships, regardless of their nature—spouse/spouse, parents/children, employer/employee, employee/customer, friend/friend—are all either getting better or getting worse. They can't just sit there; they are dynamic, changing and evolving. We are all learning, either on purpose or by accident; but as each day passes, we become different, better or more unique in some way.

Think about the last conflict you had with someone. I'll guarantee that it was most likely a trivial issue that got blown out of proportion for some reason.

The major contributor to breakdowns in communication is a person's perceptual outlook or mental filter. Each of us filters what we see and hear through a very individual set of parameters. These parameters are the result of years of experience, thoughts, impressions, learning, decisions, outcomes and all the stuff that people—parents, schools, churches, relatives, friends, colleagues and supervisors—have thrown into our filters. Often we are not even aware of how something that someone says or does influences us in the present, let alone years after the words were spoken or actions taken.

For example, if an Uncle Bob once told you that you would never be successful because no one in the family history had been—well, this simple statement, what I call mental data, is now permanently stored in your unconscious. How about a quick lesson in brain physiology?

A computer functions a lot like the human brain except that it isn't quite as effective in many ways; but the similarities in terms of activity and success are an important concept to grasp. Let me explain.

A computer has two primary elements, the hard drive and the RAM. The hard drive is where the information and software programs are stored. These programs allow the computer to function simultaneously in many ways, basically multitasking. If you don't have a particular program on your hard drive, you can't perform those functions.

Here's the problem: If you have a virus or a lot of garbage on your hard drive, or have too much going on in your RAM, the computer is slower and less productive. So, what's the comparison to your brain?

Your brain has in excess of 100 billion brain cells. There are over 1 trillion chemical reactions in the human brain every second. The brain is made up of two primary elements: the conscious and the unconscious mind. The unconscious mind automatically controls over 90% of all bodily functions without your conscious awareness: heart rate, digestion, body temperature, etc. You don't have to consciously think about these to make them happen.

Here's the problem: If you have too much clutter or viruses in your mind, it will have a negative impact on your thinking, emotions, feelings and many other human functions like decisions, behavior, reactions, etc.

So, what's on your hard drive (unconscious mind)? Well, most of the stuff in it was put there not by you, but by others: parents, friends, bosses, teachers, church leaders, etc. Your brain never forgets. Everything you have ever felt, experienced, done, not done, decided, etc., is permanently stored in your unconscious. So if a parent or uncle once told you, *you'll never amount to anything*, it's stored permanently. If a spouse has ever said, *you are worthless*—yep, it's stored for future use. If you have ever made a bad decision, you guessed it: stored. So what does all of this have to do with success, peace, happiness or effective communication?

Think about it: A lot of the stuff that's stored in your mind are the negatives you have ever experienced, thought or done; it's just like your computer has a virus. And the outcome? You are less effective, slower and lose control of the quality of your life.

Here's the key to future happiness and success: You have to control what your mind is exposed to. You have to learn to turn off the negatives and allow the positives to direct your life. How would you do this with a computer? Any or all of three ways:

1. Upgrade a software program so your computer operates at peak capacity.
2. Buy a new software program so you can use this functionality.
3. Delete unused software programs, files or junk from your computer.

Here's the challenge when it comes to the brain. You can't delete anything that has been placed in it through a variety of input methods or sources such as early conditioning, previous teaching and lessons or experiences, but you can teach the brain to override much of this previous conditioning with new information.

1. Upgrade your mental software by exposing yourself to new information—through books, seminars, training, etc.
2. You are can do different kinds of therapy to eliminate the negative software that's running, but that goes beyond the scope of this book or my expertise.

But there is an additional factor that must be considered with this approach. Just a single exposure to new information isn't enough to guarantee your brain will give you access to this information when you need it. Why? Because it depends on the overall content of the brain. If you have a lot of negative stuff in your mind, you can't upgrade or override this old information with only one exposure. The key to allowing your brain to help you succeed is REPETITION, REPETITION, REPITITION. Got it? The frequency with which the brain is exposed to information, whether positive or negative, determines which information has control of attitudes, feelings and behavior.

So, if you want to ensure that you give yourself every opportunity for success and happiness, the key is REPITITION of the material that is in your long-term best interests.

An additional benefit of REPITITION is speed. The more the mind is exposed to the same information, the faster it processes this information. For example: If, during a challenging time in your life or when you have to make an important decision, you have previously had repeated exposure to information that helps you overcome these negative circumstances, doubts or fears, the mind will bring the appropriate positive information to your conscious mind (the RAM) to help you get through this faster and easier.

If you have ever struggled with a decision, it's because the mind is processing every available memory, outcome, action and thought associated with any and all previous decisions, thereby bringing all of this previous information into the present (the RAM) while you are trying to make this new decision. Not necessarily a recipe for success, especially when accuracy or urgency is important. I'm not talking here about making faster decisions, but allowing the mind to process the current information without distraction from any negatives from the past.

Let's use a sports example. If you play tennis and practice your backswing for an hour every day, do you think that over time you will just hit the ball correctly without having to think about all of the details? It's like driving a car: When you learned, you had to pay attention to every movement and position, like rolling down the window while moving forward; but now, most of this is on 'automatic'.

Without help, you can't turn off the negatives. But you can overpower and replace them with the positives. Simple? Yes. Easy? No. Required? Absolutely.

I'll close with a simple question: What are you allowing into your brain with repetition? Worry, fear, uncertainty, frustration, stress, anxiety, anger or guilt? Or rather: possibilities, confidence, optimism, courage, personal power, joy, appreciation, patience and love?

Let me REPEAT: What you are getting in your life right now, have in the past and will in the future, is exactly what you have repeatedly allowed, based on what information has had access to your brain, because what's in your brain drives your thoughts.

Do you want a different outcome?

Then change what's gaining access to your brain. Change what you are being exposed to. Change what you are learning. Change what you are mentally focusing or concentrating on. Start exposing yourself to what you want, not what you don't want.

Back to Uncle Bob. We're assuming that his intent was not malicious; he was just being Uncle Bob. He could have been a parent or a teacher—doesn't matter.

My father once asked me after I had written my first book, *Soft Sell*, that since it wasn't selling all that well, why was I working on my second book, *The Ancient Scrolls*? Further, he said that I would never be a great writer, so I should just stop dreaming and writing and get a regular job. Well, 30 years later, sales of *Soft Sell* are now over 1,000,000 copies worldwide and since then, I have written over 80 books. Had I listened to him, I would never have written my second book or be working on this one.

He wasn't being mean. I believe that in his eyes, he was trying to be helpful and loving. But what a way to show it, to try and shut down someone's dream.

We've all been there, on the giving and/or receiving end: a word or advice spoken without regard for the years of impact it will have on a person's life.

So, what's the answer?

Keep reading. I'll share stories, examples, illustrations and personal experiences that will help you add congruence to your words and actions, as well as help you see the disconnect between another's words and their actions.

Lies, white lies, fibs and half-truths

I'll guarantee that sooner or later everyone will tell a lie, a white lie, a fib or at the minimum, a half-truth. Let's define each of these so we are all on the same page, so that I can give this topic its due.

What is truth?

A statement that corresponds to fact or reality.

Truth is. The problem is that many people believe that THEIR version of the truth is THE truth. For example, if you believed the world was flat even though it was round, your version of truth was based on hearsay, myth, rumor or misunderstanding.

What if it had been proven that the world was round, but you didn't get the message, so you still believed the world was flat?

Or, what if the world is round and you, for whatever reason, just choose to continue to believe that the world is flat?

See the problem here? Truth for you can depend on so many nebulous things like prejudices, ignorance, conditioned upbringing, arrogance, ego, fear or just plain stubbornness.

What if you are having a conversation with someone about the shape of the world and you both have different viewpoints, neither of which is grounded in realty? Guess what the outcome will be. Right: conflict, invalidation of each other for your beliefs, defensiveness, confusion or misunderstanding. More on this topic later.

What is an out-and-out lie?

To say something that is not true in a conscious effort to deceive somebody.

A lie is a deliberate attempt to mislead someone or misrepresent what you know is true and for whatever reason you are unwilling or afraid to deal in reality or truth.

How about a fib or a white lie?

A fib: an insignificant or harmless lie.

A white lie: a lie not intended to harm someone, but told in order to avoid distress, humiliation, embarrassment or personal degradation.

So, the difference is simply whether the words avoid personal pain of some kind or are just said to avoid a possible conflict or disagreement. I'm sure you have been asked by someone, "Do I look good in this outfit?" and to avoid getting into it, you say *yes* when you're really not sure. Okay, fib or white lie? A fib.

Are white lies really harmless? Well, it depends. Say your spouse asks how you think they look in a certain outfit, and you feel they look 'not so good', but you know that's not what they want to hear, so you tell them they look 'great'. What's the harm in this? Again, it depends on the circumstances.

If your partner asks you if you like the meal they made and you hate it, but you tell them you liked it because you don't want to hurt their feelings since they spent so much time preparing it—well, guess what? You're most likely going to get that meal again in the future and have to struggle through your dislike once again with poise and discomfort.

So, what's a half-truth?

A statement that includes only some of the relevant facts or information and so is intended or likely to be misleading.

Ever told a half-truth? What's a half-truth? Well, it's leaving something out of your message. You didn't completely lie with what you said, but is telling only half the truth as bad as telling a lie? Well, again, it depends.

Here's an example.

Let's say your spouse asks you why you were late coming home from work. You respond, "I had to work late." Now, let's also assume that you did have to work late, but stopped off to meet a few friends for an after-work drink, and you conveniently left that out of your response to your spouse. Did you tell the truth? Yes. But did you tell the whole truth? No. But you say, "Well, I can't go giving my spouse a blow-by-blow description of what I did moment-by-moment when he or she asks, 'How was your day?'"

Yes, you are right. Some people want more details than others when questions like this are asked. But the real issue here is integrity. Let's go back to the previous conversation for a minute. What if later that evening, he or she asked, "Did you do anything after work before you came home?" Right here is the crux of the difference between a half- truth and the whole truth. If you feel uncomfortable telling him or her the rest of the story, you obviously felt that telling them the whole story earlier might have conjured up some conflict, so you left that part out of your answer. It comes back to your reasons, intent or rationales. If you leave out stuff that you hope people won't discover later for any reason, that's a half-truth.

A lie? No. But a misrepresentation? You betcha.

Why do people tell half-truths? Fear? Uncertainty of the other person's reaction? Insecurity? The intent to hide something? An attempt to be compassionate or understanding? *Yes* to all of these reasons. But are some of them healthier than others? Of course. If your partner asks how you like their outfit and you think it looks ugly, do you just tell them the truth? First of all, everything is in the eye of the beholder. You may think it's ugly, but you could also be in the minority about this.

Let's say your partner were to ask ten people what they thought of their outfit. Do you think they might get a variety of responses? Yes. So, who's right? Saying you like something when you don't is your personal opinion. If your partner wants your opinion, they will ask. However, if they are insecure and want validation, and you fail to give it to them, well, *'Katy, bar the door!'*

I am by no means suggesting that fibbing, lying or misrepresentations are good, healthy or even wise; but I am suggesting that you need to know what your partner expects when they ask a question like this. I can also tell you that if you continue to appease them, when that isn't what they want or need from you, sooner or later you will regret it.

What's the answer when it comes to all of these departures from the full truth?

Truth sometimes hurts, but the hurt will usually be far less uncomfortable, over time, than misrepresenting anything and having to deal with both the internal stress and external remembering to act in accordance with any lie, fib or half-truth.

Mark Twain once said, "If you tell the truth, you don't have to remember anything." How true.

How are relationships impacted in terms of words vs. actions or behavior?

One of the major problems in any relationship, personal or business, is the issue of communication or what I call the exchange of information. How information is shared or communicated and interpreted is a function of timing, method, emotions, feelings, agendas and expectations; but the words themselves and how they are linked together are the real crux when it comes to clarity and integrity.

For example, if you are having a conversation with a customer, and they ask, "When can I expect a response to [whatever]?" And you say, "I'll get back to you as soon as I have an answer or I am able." What are the problems with this response?

1. For starters, when is *as soon as I can?* You see, all communication is not just about giving words to others, but how you mean them and how others interpret them.
2. Another problem is that it can send a message that other things you are working on are more important than responding to the customer's need. Now, I'm not judging what is or isn't more important in terms of your priorities; but the subtle message could be, *you're not that important to me*, or *your issue is not high on my list of priorities.*
3. Another problem here could be that maybe I am not the person you should be dealing with for this issue; but, for whatever reason, I let you assume I am—which keeps you 'wondering'.

Any or all of these and other scenarios are possible just because of this simple phrase, *as soon as I can.*

Communication between two people is never easy and is riddled with potential for misinterpretation or misunderstanding. Not to mention the potential for assumptions that any of us can make regarding another person's words.

Assumption: something that is believed to be true without proof.

Ever assumed something? Ever had someone assume something different than your intended message? This happens every day in every relationship unless there is a systematic communication technique that is used to eliminate any or all assumptions that we or others make.

There is only one way to eliminate an assumption and it is this: After you say, promise or commit to something, you then ask the other person how they understand what you said. It might take a few extra minutes of communication, but this clarity will all but ensure that assumptions are never made; and if they are, they are disarmed sooner rather than later.

Let's go back to the previous conversation.

The salesperson says to you, "I'll get back to you as soon as I can."

Your choices are:

1. Assume it will be sooner rather than later.
2. Assume that they are serious about getting to it quickly.
3. Assume that they say this to everyone and you have just been set up.

The possible assumptions here will depend on a variety of factors:

1. how important this is to you,
2. what else is going on in your life or career at this point,
3. how you expect to be treated,
4. and/or how you have been treated in the past by others in similar positions.

So, what's the answer to eliminating frustration, stress, assumptions, confusion, misunderstanding and even anger in these situations?

Use a simple follow-up question or request:

- "Please tell me what you mean by [x-time].
- "What do you mean by, *as soon as you can?"*
- "When is *as soon as you can?"*

Having an integrity-based follow-up process to any communication is one of the best ways to reduce or eliminate the potential for uncertainty, frustration or misunderstanding.

The truth, the whole truth and nothing but the truth

We've seen enough movies, or perhaps had the experience in a courtroom where someone is to be sworn in as a witness. This person is asked under oath, "Do you swear to tell the truth, the whole truth and nothing but the truth, so help you God?"

Most of us don't have to give sworn testimony on a regular basis, but every day we are presented with opportunities to tell the truth—or not.

Truth is often hard. Why?

For starters, the inability to be truthful often comes from insecurity, fear, uncertainty or a personal or hidden agenda. It's often easier to couch the truth with some untruth in order to justify that we didn't out-and-out lie, because a portion of our message was actually true.

For example, if your spouse asks, "Why do you love me?"

"Well, I love you because you ____________." But, what if there are things you don't love or like about him or her, as well as those you do. Do you include these in your response or conveniently leave them out because that wasn't part of the question?

See where I am going here?

Or, let's say your boss asks you to evaluate his or her ability or performance as a manger?

Do you give them the good, the bad and the ugly—or just the good? It depends on

- how you think they will react to your response;
- or, based on past experience, whether they really want all three;
- or, if voicing all three could put your job or career in jeopardy.

These kinds of questions are never simple, and the answers will always (for most people) depend on any number of factors, as I have stated.

If you want truth and nothing but the truth, you need a safe emotional environment, a respectful relationship and the courage and ability to share truth, regardless of how you feel it might be perceived or interpreted.

What are the consequences of the truth?

The truth can often hurt, not because we don't necessarily like what we are hearing, but because it sometimes surprises us or is not what we wanted to hear.

I have had to deliver bad news to clients, children, spouses and employees over the years, telling them what they didn't want to hear or least expected. This is never easy as a manager, parent, spouse or even friend. We all want to hear good news, validating feedback and positive and reinforcing words about our abilities, opportunities, results or even our efforts.

But sooner or later, everyone is disappointed by someone in their life who has broken a promise, didn't meet an obligation or just had a simple 'senior moment'. This is normal; we are all human, and none of us is perfect. We all make mistakes and we are all guilty from time to time of saying things or offering things we don't mean or can't deliver.

However, when you always come from a position of truth, you'll be amazed at how others will react to you, even though your message may be unpopular or unexpected.

It's really quite simple: If you will always come from truth, not your truth, but truth, you'll never have to worry about wondering what to say next or how to say it. Not always an easy task, given what I have previously shared.

Remember that life is perceptual, and when you share 'your' truth with someone—an opinion, a judgment, an observation, etc.—this is still 'your' opinion and it doesn't necessarily mean it's true for anyone else. Ask any ten people what they think about something, and you will get a variety of answers. So, what exactly is truth? Keep reading.

What are the benefits of truth?

Truth in the long term is the best strategy, no matter how painful it might appear to be when you are telling it. But keep in mind that everyone's version of truth can vary. This doesn't mean that people lie from time to time; just that as they grow, in many ways their version of truth can and will evolve.

The benefits of truth are many. Here are just a few of the obvious ones:

1. Less stress
2. Less disappointment over time
3. Communication clarity
4. Better relationships
5. Greater inner peace
6. Less inner emotional turmoil
7. Relationships grounded in trust and respect
8. Greater respect from others
9. Increased emotional courage
10. Less worry

Although truth may on the surface appear to be difficult and challenging at times, in the longer term it is always the best policy for integrity-based relationships.

What could be some potential negatives of truth?

It might appear, based on the above, that truth may occasionally bring with it some apparent negatives for the short-term. So, you have to decide whether you want to have short-term peace or comfort from the temporary satisfaction or acceptance of your messages or whether you would rather deal with the short-term fear for the benefit of the long-term peace, congruence and happiness that comes with authenticity.

Having said this, there might on the surface appear to be some negatives to telling the truth; things like:

- Disapproval
- Conflict
- Disappointment
- Hurt Feelings
- Anger
- Frustration
- Uncertainty

But in the long run, these short-term emotions or reactions are nothing when compared to carrying the negative consequences of not telling the truth with you for months or even years. But remember: Truth is often just your opinion and not a 'cut in stone' truth.

Is truth ever not true?

Truth—what is it? I could give you hundreds of examples, but two will explain my thoughts on this topic. For centuries, the majority of world citizens believed the world was flat when, in fact, it was round. To these people, this was a truth based on commonly accepted, although incorrect, knowledge that was available to them at the time. Just because everyone believed it, didn't make it true. It took exploration to finally dispel this myth and change people's view or version of truth regarding this subject. Just because you think or believe something is true, doesn't mean it is. Each of us has our version of a multitude of truths when, in reality, these are just opinions or personal perceptions.

Second example: Scientists believed for years that the smallest particle was an atom. This truth, as far as they were concerned, was grounded in past and current scientific research, discovery and investigation. Ask a scientist at that time, "Is the atom the smallest particle?" and their answer would have been *yes*. Flash forward to the invention of the electron microscope, and BAM – the atom is not the smallest particle after all. So, what is truth? Is it just a temporary mindset or is it grounded in something greater?

The speed of light and the law of gravity are truths that have been true for centuries. But consider: Could there be something else hidden in the wings that will dispel these laws, which just hasn't been discovered yet?

Just because you believe something is true doesn't make it true. A perfect example is an assumption. You assume something is true based on your experience, knowledge, opinions or history, but this doesn't make it true. And, I'll bet today you have made at least one assumption, and whether it turns out to be true or not depends . . . .

Why people fudge their words

Hurt feelings

No one, generally, wants to hurt another's feelings. Yes, there are some nasty, unpleasant and hurtful people out there, but I believe most people usually have compassionate motives when they communicate with others. Often, people say hurtful things when under stress, anxiety, pain or any other negative emotion; but when people come from a position of love, they may hurt others with their words, but this was not their intent.

So, why do so many people fudge their message or leave stuff out of their communication, for fear of hurting another person's feelings or to avoid conflict?

Is it because of insecurity, poor emotional maturity or some hidden agenda or other purpose? A great question.

When was the last time someone hurt your feelings by what they said? When was the last time someone edited a message to avoid hurting your feelings? When was the last time you did either of these?

Sooner or later we will all edit a message to someone to avoid a conflict or postpone a disappointment. If you have ever done either, welcome to the human race. The key here is, is it done routinely, for fear of the consequences, or is it done spontaneously as a knee-jerk reaction to a request or something someone said to you?

What exactly are hurt feelings?

It's simply when someone says something you didn't expect and you choose to take what they said in a negative way or it causes you to feel temporarily unworthy or inadequate in some way.

No one can know what is in another person's mind and how they will respond to every single word or message that is shared or communicated. We all filter what we hear based on what we want to hear, believe, expect or desire.

So, if I tell you, "You look happy," and you feel like I should have said, "You look beautiful", what I said wasn't wrong or bad, but it wasn't what you wanted to hear or expected. Thus, a temporary disappointment causing your feelings to be hurt.

If you said to me, "You did a nice job with that project," and I was expecting, "You did a tremendous job with that project," the result is the same: I didn't hear what I wanted.

Hurt feelings are not just when people say things that make us feel insecure or invalidated, but when what is said is not what we expected.

What is the cause of hurt feelings? Is it what is said or how it's said, or not what was expected? It can be any or all three. Here's the crux of this situation: I can't control what you say or how you say it, but I can control, if I choose to, how I hear it or how I choose to react to your words.

Conflict

Conflict is normal in any relationship. Sooner or later there is going to be disagreement, disconnect or differences of opinion. It's impossible for two humans in any relationship, personal or business, to agree on everything all of the time. This is a simple reality based on the differences in education, upbringing, experience, attitudes and life outlook. So, the real challenge when it comes to words and their contribution to conflict is the ability to disarm the conflict in advance with better communication, therefore reducing its negative impact on the quality of the relationship.

This takes compassion, letting go of ego control, a willingness to see a subject from a different perspective and the ability to let go of or better manage personal opinions, prejudices, expectations or agendas.

If one or both people in a relationship come to a discussion without this ability or willingness, conflict is ensured. It's not always the words that cause the conflict between two people, but a person's unique interpretation of the words used in any dialog. Yes, many people have negative agendas and express them with the intent of exploitation or manipulation. But when two people are generally willing to see any subject without blind spots or hidden agendas, a potential conflict can actually improve a relationship.

Is this a contradiction? Actually, no.

Every person in a relationship has certain stuff they keep to themselves. Some of this is unimportant trivia, while some of it could slowly or quickly destroy a relationship's trust, respect, compassion or understanding if it never gets to the surface to be openly discussed. Often conflict can be a trigger that gets this out in the open, allowing you to discuss and yes, even argue about it; but at least it's now on the table. If your relationship is grounded in trust and respect, you will most likely be able to address the issue in a productive way, even if there are some short-term hurt feelings.

These short-term reactions are better for the relationship's success than one or both of you harboring hidden issues that require your continual effort and energy to keep hidden. By the way, hiding them will sooner or later have an indirect impact on many other relationship issues or topics, because they will become a negative filter through which other subjects must pass, subjects which may be solvable; but they will be harder to deal with, given that you are hanging onto the concealed blockages.

Since all relationships have conflict, the key to better relationships isn't necessarily the conflicts themselves, but the ability to manage the conflicts in a positive and respectful way, thereby improving the overall climate and impact of communication.

Fear

Fear is the number one contributor to breakdowns in communication, regardless of the circumstances. Fear has many faces: the need for acceptance, the desire for validation, the concern for being right and the fear of losing control over one's life, for instance.

Fear is the root of all arguments, misunderstandings, conflicts and assumptions.

Why?

No one likes to be wrong. The problem is that being right or wrong is more a function of personal attachment to attitudes, beliefs, values and opinions than to what is actually true. Conventional wisdom, mindsets, personal experience and paradigms are generally well-embedded in a person's mind and, therefore, contribute to their feelings, attitudes, behavior and how they express themselves, as well as how they interpret what they hear.

When a person comes from a fear-centered rather than a love-centered position, they will almost always be in a defensive posture, protecting their need to be right, to know or to be better in some way. Arrogance, defensiveness, insecurity, guilt, anger, resentment and defensiveness are all rooted in fear.

Stress

When people are experiencing a high level stress for any reason, their communication will tend to become more guarded, less open and honest and more prone to argument and conflict.

Stress dramatically impacts how the mind and body function.

The reason stress is the number one contributor to all illness, sickness and disease is simply because this stress keeps the body, through the mind, in a flight, fight or freeze protective state, thereby robbing other bodily functions such as blood pressure, digestion or the ability to resist disease, of the nutrients they need to function properly. As a side note: The brain uses over 25% of the body's nutrition, so is it any wonder why people are tired when they are under stress, anxious, worried or are struggling with a life decision?

People under stress focus not on long-term, but short-term consequences and solutions to their problems or challenges. As a result, they may say or do things that, if they had spent more time considering the consequences of their words or actions, they may have held back or better composed their statements, responses, promises or commitments.

Stress is a killer. This is a proven medical fact; but what I am concerned with here is how stress is a relationship killer due the communication patterns that erupt because of it.

The essential thing to consider when it comes to stress and communication, whether verbal or non-verbal, is that you will say and do things that will most likely hamper open and congruent communication, thereby sending mixed messages to the other person.

These mixed messages can be totally contradictory to what you really feel or believe.

To avoid these negative outcomes during times of stress, it is necessary to take time to relax, pause, reflect and consider your words and actions rather than just 'knee-jerking' your way through a conversation or behavioral response.

Emotional Immaturity

Just because someone has hit the ripe old age of fifty or even eighty doesn't mean they are emotionally mature when it comes to communication, behavior or intent.

I know many people who at an early age, due to their upbringing and experiences, are more emotionally mature than someone twice their age. So, what exactly is emotional immaturity?

Here's a formal definition for you: being by nature easily affected by or quick to express emotions.

Emotional maturity or the lack of it means simply that a person either has control over their emotions and their contributors or they don't.

For example: Someone says something to intentionally hurt your feelings, and you now have a choice: to react (act again) the way you typically would in this type of situation—or—you can make a conscious choice that you are not going to let this other person control your reactions, responses or emotions by pushing your emotional buttons.

Simply put, emotional maturity is when you respond emotionally because of choice and self-control. If you get angry, it's because you have chosen to allow this behavior. If you cry while watching a sad or emotionally-charged movie, it's done as an accepted behavior and not because it's expected by others.

We all have our 'emotional buttons'. Typically, most people let others determine their behavior (words or responses). Many people in our lives know what to do or say to get us charged, upset, motivated, angry—whatever. Here's the problem: When we respond based on what we heard rather than from an inner place of emotional control, we have now turned our emotional world over to others. If this becomes typical behavior, we will tend to lose total control of who we are and how we behave. It doesn't matter whether it's due to a traffic jam or the toxic words of a spouse or even a total stranger.

Emotional maturity is self-control. It's the ability to decide how you will behave and when and why.

This doesn't mean that you won't ever flare up with anger, upset or disappointment; but when you do it will be from an inner center ruled by choice and not from someone or something pushing your buttons.

Uncertainty

Oswald Chambers said it: "The only thing that is certain in life is its uncertainty."

Uncertainty can contribute to stress, fear, disappointment, discouragement and inaction—all of which will influence a person's words and behavior.

When we allow uncertainty to rule our lives, we will most likely come from a position of un-control. This lack of perceived control over a person's circumstances and life outcomes will almost invariably cause breakdowns in communication and a lack of integrity in their words and deeds.

Why?

For starters, when we feel insecure in the areas of our safety, security, happiness or health, we will almost always bring a lack of congruence to the conversations with others and inconsistency to our behaviors.

Generally speaking, most people want to communicate with honesty and openness; but when life throws us a curve, we will almost always come from a position of fear. When fear rules a person's life, it will have a tremendous negative impact on all of their actions, thoughts, words and behaviors.

When you are in a flight, flee or freeze state of mind, you will be responding to life from the mental position of panic; and when in a panic state of mind, you will convince yourself that your actions are justified.

Here is a real life example to illustrate this issue.

You have just lost your job and are concerned about your ability to cover your basic expenses. As the weeks pass and you have not secured a new position, your funds are running out and the future looks bleak, despair begins to overcome your ability to make sound long- or even short-term decisions.

You are finally offered a new job, one that just doesn't feel right to accept, but it will temporarily solve your financial needs. Your inner guidance system keeps telling you, "Don't take the position; be patient, all will be well." But your panic says, "Take it." So, what do you do? You will generally take it.

I have been in this position and I can tell you: Every morning that I woke up after I began that new position, I had this knot in my stomach and an ache in my heart, knowing it just wasn't right. Within a few days of choosing to leave that position (and doing so), the daily pain was gone, my creativity kicked in and I was able to find alternative ways to solve this financial challenge that felt right and ultimately worked.

Is the issue despair, discouragement, anxiety, stress or uncertainty—or—is it a lack of faith, belief and confidence in yourself and life?

Think about some decisions you have made when in panic (despair, discouragement, frustration, etc.), and I'll bet they didn't work out well for the long term.

There are literally millions of things that can cause us to not honor our promises or commitments (statements of intent), and these things are just a part of life as it unfolds day by day.

For example:

1. I promised you I would pay this bill, but the money I expected to cover this expense didn't appear—and I ended up breaking my promise.
2. I said I would get this project done on time, but got the flu—so I wasn't able to deliver.
3. I promised I would be on time, but a traffic accident had cars backed up for miles and there was nothing I could do—so I was late.

So, what are we to do?

We can either accept the consequences when we tell someone that something absolutely will or won't happen—or—we can be proactive by blending the realities of life and its uncertainty into all of our promises and commitments: "I'll do the best I can to take care of... be on time... do what I said I would do," etc.

Ego

When a person's ego takes over in a relationship, all communication will be prejudiced and calculated. Know anyone with an 'out of control' ego? Or in the extreme, a 'control freak'? If you do, you know that whatever they say or tell you usually has some self-serving agenda.

A person's ego needs them to be in control and for them to always look better or smarter than the other person, and to appear more successful, regardless of their career, ability, experience, knowledge, status or position.

These people will say anything as long as they feel it serves their personal needs.

In a relationship, whether personal or business, with someone with a huge ego, you will seldom win a discussion or even an argument. With them, it's not about what's right or good or even true; they must be right, no matter what.

People with large egos—keep in mind we all have an ego—will be difficult to communicate with in an open and honest way.

The key to the congruence between words and behavior with 'big ego people' is to accept that you will hardly ever be right, so trying to influence or persuade them or even have a simple conversation about a simple topic will often be a challenging experience.

You can seldom prove them wrong, beat them, or even have them respect your opinion (no matter how correct) if it differs from theirs.

Arrogance

Arrogance: behavior or attitudes that demonstrate that you think or believe you are better or more important than or superior to other people.

Arrogance is a form of stubbornness or an unwillingness to see things from a different perspective. It can be rooted in insecurity, pride, haughtiness or ego.

When a person comes from a mindset of arrogance, they will seldom be willing to accept a viewpoint different from their own, regardless of how this opinion or truth is rooted in accuracy.

If you work with or for an arrogant person, you will hardly ever win a discussion or even have it remain neutral. In most cases, you will end up in a defensive posture unless you are willing to see and accept their side of the story.

When conversing with an arrogant person, you will almost always come away feeling less worthy, invalidated or insecure; that is; if you let them have this kind of control over your views, beliefs or feelings.

You can't turn an arrogant person into something they are not, as their arrogance is usually rooted in some deeper emotional need, in fear or lack of self-acceptance. These people do not come from a position of 'reality', but their 'own reality', right or wrong.

Personal agendas

Everyone has agendas; some are noble, while others can be very self-serving.

Whether it involves dating, long-term relationships, customers or employees, friends or relatives, sooner or later a person's agenda will surface in a conversation, behavior or just life in general.

An agenda is simply a reason for doing or saying something or not doing it or saying it. There can be numerous reasons why a person has an agenda, which can vary from individual to individual.

A person can have one agenda with a spouse or friend and a totally different one with an employee, supervisor or customer. For example:

- You can have a career agenda to achieve success even at the expense of a personal relationship with a spouse or children.
- At the same time, your actual lived agenda with family does not support your career agenda.

In other words, you can say you want success at any cost, but often put the needs or expectations of family ahead of these career agendas. This creates conflict within yourself, as well as with your career and also your family.

These agendas in and of themselves are not necessarily good or bad, but often depend on the person's subtle or overt intention. Even though a person may try to hide their agendas, sooner or later they will usually surface in attitudes, behavior and/or words.

Tension level

Everyone is in one of five tension (emotional) states at all times. These states are a function of two elements in a person's life: their perceived challenges and their perceived resources.

The five tension states are: Stress, Power Stress, Power, Power Apathy and Apathy. If a person's perceived challenges are high and their perceived resources are low, they will tend to be in the Stress tension state. If their perceived resources are high and their perceived challenges low, they will tend to be in the Apathy emotional state.

What does all of this have to do with communication, behavior and a person's words vs. their actions?

If a person is in the Stress emotional state, they will usually feel out of control, be in a panic mode, and will say or do whatever they need to or have to, to reduce their stress. In other words, there will be little integrity or connection between their words and deeds.

If a person is in Apathy, they will tend not to communicate at all as this tends to be the 'sleeping while you are awake' state. In this case, they will be poor listeners and have a 'who cares?' attitude about what is being discussed.

If you want congruent communication between two people, it is important to be aware of the state both you and the other person are in, in order to anticipate the connection between words and behavior.

The positive state for congruency and effective communication is Power Stress. In this state, people feel they are in control and will tend to listen and attempt to understand others. This doesn't mean they will agree with or like the message, only that they hear it because, for whatever reason, they are interested.

Lack of information or knowledge

There is a significant difference between information, knowledge and wisdom.

We are all generally overloaded with information today, thanks to the Internet and technology; but just because you have access to more information than you can ever assimilate doesn't mean you will use it wisely. Learning to distinguish between available information and what is actually relevant to your life is a totally different challenge.

It is estimated that the average person today spends in excess of 58 hours per month on the Internet.

Granted, your mind has an incredible amount of storage space and processing ability, so this isn't the problem. What is, is deciding which information is appropriate to living a full, happy and balanced life.

Knowledge comes as a result of study and contemplation.

Wisdom is the ability to use what you have been exposed to, learned and put to use in a productive and appropriate way to improve your life style, career, relationships or any other area of your life.

Information will not improve your life. Knowledge can, if it is turned into wisdom.

So, friends, how does all of this impact communication, conversation and behavior?

For starters, just because you know a lot or are even wise is no guarantee that you will be willing to share what you have learned in an effective way.

- Ever had a conversation with someone who was brilliant, but was unable to express himself or herself accurately?
- Ever had a conversation with someone who was really smart, but used this intelligence for their personal agendas?
- Ever had a conversation with a well-informed person who mis-represented what they knew for their own benefit?

These are just a few of the many scenarios when it comes to information, knowledge and wisdom, and the ability to communicate with understanding, compassion and integrity.

Lack of experience

The saying goes, "Experience is the best teacher." However, just because experience is a good teacher doesn't mean that everyone is a good student.

Think about it. Our experience is the direct result of our choices, actions, behavior and decisions, as well as who and what we were exposed to during our personal history, whether negative or positive. However, just because you made what you believed was a bad decision and ended up with what you thought was a negative outcome, keep in mind that it's not the outcomes that determine who we are and how we behave, but what we do with these outcomes or how we interpret them.

Experience can be a wonderful teacher if we have a mindset that sees all experience as an opportunity to learn and grow.

Let's say you learned from an early life-experience to never trust anyone. You will tend to bring this mindset to all of the new people you meet from then on or until you learn not to let this paradigm determine all of your encounters. The choice is yours about how to interpret or apply this lesson.

Let's say you failed at something when you attempted a new project, activity or initiative. As a result, the feedback from others was, "Don't try again because you'll have the same results." If you let this feedback rule your actions, you will most likely remain stuck in this life philosophy.

How will your experiences contribute to your communication and actions with others?

Suppose you meet a new person that you are attracted to and you would like to pursue a possible relationship with them. So, you meet, talk, share and learn. But then the other person says certain things that bring up 'red flags' as you compare their words with those of others who said similar things. Your mindset of mistrust, your mind and emotions will now be on 'high alert'. Will this have a bearing on how you relate to this new person? What do you think?

The key when meeting new people or having a conversation with anyone is to bring a clean mental and emotional slate to the encounter. However, most people are unable to do this; thus they tend to let their history determine their future. This is a recipe for continued conflict, judgment, disappointment and stress in any relationship.

Integrity-based words

As I have said numerous times, words are just words; but what gives each word or phrase its meaning or interpretation depends entirely on a wide variety of factors that are not within the control of the person sending a message. So, what are integrity-based words?

When I refer to *integrity-based words,* I am referring to ensuring that the message sent is congruent with the intent of the person sending the message, regardless of the speaker's tone or timing, or the listener's acceptance or circumstances. It's not whether the recipient likes the message, agrees with the message or is comfortable with it. All that matters is that they hear it and are able to mentally process it consistent with the intent of the message you sent.

When a supervisor asks for your opinion, and you know from experience that what they really want is what they want to hear and not your opinion, you have a choice: Tell them what they want to hear, even though you know it in no way represents what you believe, think or feel—or risk some negative feedback or consequence by telling them your real feelings or beliefs.

When a spouse asks you what you think about something, anything—if you know that telling them what you really think will contribute to a conflict, you again have a choice: Patronize them with what you know will be a neutral response, thereby avoiding a conflict—or tell them like it is from your perspective and then handle any conflict that may show up.

What if you ask one of your kids a simple, *why did you do that?* Now they have to consider, based on their limited education and experience, what is going to be an acceptable answer that won't lead to a time-out!

Before I move deeper into this section, here's a definition of *integrity*: the quality of possessing and steadfastly adhering to high moral principles or professional standards, ethics and consistent behavior.

Integrity in communication can mean many different things to people because their integrity or lack of it will often be grounded in their experience and the mindsets that have been developed, modified or changed during their life, due to both external influence and their inner interpretation of those influences.

Everyone will define integrity uniquely, depending on their agendas, goals, lifestyle, challenges, expectations and current circumstances.

- Ever had an argument with a spouse where he or she didn't see things the way you did or you wanted them to?
- Ever had a conflict with a customer or colleague because they wouldn't see the situation the way you wanted them or needed them to?
- Ever had a disagreement with a supervisor because their interpretation of a policy or procedure differed from how you viewed the policy or procedure?

Every day there are literally billions of disagreements, assumptions, misunderstandings and conflicts that lead to relationship stress as well as broken relationships, due to people's inability to successfully resolve them in a respectful and compassionate way.

Many of these negative outcomes could have been reduced or avoided entirely if they had been managed in a more proactive and understanding manner.

So, what does it take to do that?

Here is one technique that can help improve the understanding of a message and its intent, while at the same time improving communication clarity and the congruence between words and behaviors.

Use a Talking Stick

There are a number of Native American traditions that I have been interested in for many years. One of them that has tremendous value in communication is the use of a 'Talking Stick'.

Some of you may be wondering, *what in the world is a Talking Stick?* I don't have the space here to go into the origination of the tradition. I only want to illustrate its use and value. (By the way, you can use any symbol for a talking stick; it doesn't have to be a wooden stick or a fancy device you spent a fortune on at some gift shop during your travels.)

One of the significant problems in communication is the issue of interrupting others while they are talking. When you interrupt someone, you are saying: *You don't matter, your ideas are not important, I am not listening to you, I don't care about what you are saying, etc.* Believe me: None of these messages contributes to open, honest communication and positive relationships.

Enter, the Talking Stick. Let's say two people are having a discussion of any kind, pleasant or otherwise. (This could be a manager and his or her employee, a parent and a child over the age of 12, or two people in a personal and intimate relationship.) Person A has the Talking Stick and begins sharing their thoughts or ideas about anything: last night's dinner, something that happened at work or just aimless venting.

Person B cannot say a word, not a word, until Person A surrenders the stick. Person B can't grab it, steal it, ask for it—nothing. They must wait and say nothing (other than acknowledge Person A's points or thoughts; they just listen.) When Person A is finished expressing their opinion, idea or thought, they then pass the stick to Person B. The same rules now apply for Person A that were applicable for Person B. Person A cannot talk, not a word, until Person B surrenders the stick voluntarily to Person A. Get it?

What is the point of this stick anyway? Well, use your imagination for just a minute. What would the use of this stick do for people's willingness to listen? How would it affect the quality of the communication? It would validate the other person by sending the message that I, the listener, care about what you feel, believe or think.

This simple device can be used in a business setting such as a meeting just as easily as it can in a personal discussion. I have witnessed any number of business meetings where communication does not take place because people are more interested in what they are going to say rather than what the other person is currently saying.

If you want to improve the quality of your listening and your communication, I recommend you consider using this wonderful little device. A talking stick can be a toy, a stick from a tree in your yard, one you made, even a spoon. Granted, some of these are not as glamorous as one carved in stone from an indigenous tribe in the center of Alaska, but it's the symbolism that matters, not the implement itself. Try it, it works.

Meet people where they are

You have to meet people where they are emotionally before you can take them emotionally where you want to take them. What does this mean?

Let's say your spouse is angry—doesn't matter what it's about or what caused it—and they are expressing their anger toward you or taking it out on you even if you weren't the cause of it.

You have a choice: You can be drawn into their anger by responding defensively, protecting your ego, emotions or feelings, even though you were not the cause of their emotional outbreak —or you can choose to stay neutral.

One of the best ways to improve communication in any situation is to meet the other person where they are emotionally. This doesn't mean that you get angry also, just that you meet them with poise and understanding of the emotion they are expressing.

For example, he starts expressing angry words because of something that happened at work that day. You listen and respond with something like, "You have every right to feel the way you do; you were wronged and it wasn't right. They shouldn't have treated you that way; it was unfair."

This approach sends compassion, acceptance and understanding to the other person. It doesn't mean you agree with their view, only that you are seeing things from their perspective.

This is meeting someone where they are.

Here's another example.

Your friend is expressing fear about an unknown future event. You can show sympathy or empathy for their circumstances.

By showing *empathy*, you help people grow and see things more clearly and self-discover what they need to learn or understand to grow. By showing *sympathy* instead, you tend to help people remain stuck in their circumstances, attitudes, conditions or their victim mindset.

Meeting your friend in their fear doesn't mean you are condoning it or agreeing with their reactions or emotions; it means that you are seeing what they are seeing. You are relating to them without having to feel what they are experiencing.

Once you meet a person emotionally where they are, it's a lot easier to help them see a situation or experience from a different perspective.

Native Americans have a concept called the Medicine Wheel; they see life as circular rather than linear. In essence, this means there are many ways to see, view or interpret things. For instance, let's say you are looking at something from the three o'clock position on the Wheel. There are other ways to view this situation: from the six o'clock, ten o'clock or one o'clock position, for instance.

In any situation, everyone will look at the same circumstance or situation and view it from their particular position on the Wheel. A person viewing a challenge from the nine o'clock position will have a different perspective from someone who is experiencing the same set of circumstances from the three o'clock perspective. It's not about what is right or wrong, good or bad, positive or negative; just that there is always another way to see or experience something.

However, if a person is stuck in their perspective (e.g., the eight o'clock position) they will seldom see or be open to a different viewpoint.

Meeting someone where they are implies that you travel around the circle from your position, wherever it is, to view the situation from their position or perspective.

Once you have met them where they are, they will tend to be more willing to see the same situation in an alternative way; but you have to guide them gradually and gently to a different viewpoint or position on the Wheel.

For example, in the above situation, the spouse could have said something like, "I can see why you are upset, and this wasn't what you expected in terms of how you should be treated." (Meeting them where they are) "But have you considered that there might be another way to see this situation such as...." (Taking them where you want to take them.)

The use of questions

One of the biggest contributors to misunderstanding and conflict is when people assume that what they heard is what you meant. The best way to avoid these types of 'set-ups' is to always ask clarifying questions if you have any doubt about what someone means by their words.

For example: After our first date, I tell you I will call you to get together for lunch, but I never call. You wonder and ponder and begin to question my intent or the integrity of my words or what I said I would do.

There are two ways you can deal with this kind of statement *at the time I make it*: 1) Assume I will call and then wait and wonder, or 2) ask to set a date and/or time right then and there.

For example, you can ask:

1. "When do you want to get together for lunch?"
2. "When will you call—which day or part of the day, evening or morning? "
3. "Are you serious when you say you will call or just being nice?"
4. "Do you really want to get together for lunch? If so, let's set a date now." And so on.

These are called clarifying questions. Now, what clarifying questions could you ask about the following four issues?

1. A customer says they will email you their PO (Purchase Order).
2. An employee says they will have the report done by the end of the day.
3. A spouse says, "Let's go for a day trip this Saturday."
4. A boss says they will meet with you by the end of the week to discuss your idea.

Got the picture? Everyone makes promises or commitments they often don't mean or can't accurately control. Yes, things can come up at the last minute and yes, there are always unexpected situations. But what I'm talking about here are not those single instances, but rather behavioral or communication trends. If a parent says to their kids, "Let's go camping this weekend," but it doesn't happen, but they keep promising each weekend—finally the kids will get it: We can't trust you or believe you, because you always let something else get in the way.

Follow others' statements with questions

Let's say you are in the middle of a conversation and the other person gives you their opinion or feelings. You have two choices:

1. You can listen and then voice your own opinion.
2. You can ask them a question about what they have just said.

Let's take another look at the outcomes of the first option. When someone tells you something, and you immediately give them your own opinion, how can they interpret your response?—and I'm not talking here about the words you use, but the approach you use.

They could see your immediate response as:

- Not listening
- Not caring
- Not interested
- Not hearing

Why? Well, when someone gives you their opinion and your first response is to express your own, they can rightly interpret that you have a greater interest in what you want to say rather than in what they just shared.

When your first response to whatever they shared is a question, this approach can be interpreted in a totally different way, such as:

- You are interested.
- You do care.
- You were listening.
- You want to better understand.
- You want clarification.

With the first response above, you are indirectly invalidating the other person; with the second approach, you are validating them. So, which approach do you think will tend to foster better communication, increased communication integrity and overall better relationships?

Avoid red flags

Everyday conversations are riddled with red flags. These are often driven by fear, insecurity or some type of agenda.

Here are just a few:

- I'll do my best . . .
- I'll try . . .
- Let me be honest . . .

- When I get time . . .
- I promise . . .
- You don't understand . . .
- That's not what I meant . . .
- You can trust me . . .
- I will always . . .
- I would never . . .
- I was just kidding . . .

Here's one of my favorites: when someone says to you, "I don't mean to interrupt." And they say this as they are interrupting you. Of course they mean to interrupt you, because that is what they are doing. Saying *I don't mean to* while they are doing it just sends a contradictory message.

Why not say instead, "May I interrupt you?" Silly distinction, you say? Not at all. It shows respect and courtesy, among other things.

Words, meanings, interpretations and subtle messages are always in play in every conversation. Someone, depending on their vocabulary, education, experience or ability to articulate, might notice some of these subtle messages, while for others they just might fly over the top of their head without any notice.

Here's the vital question: Can you be sure that someone is always accurately interpreting your message in the way it was intended, based on the words you choose? The simple answer is, NO.

Of course, many of these types of phrases are said with integrity and positive intent, but too often they are just a ruse that people use to protect themselves or to mislead others.

If you are ever at the receiving end of one of these red flags, it's important to probe further to determine whether they are said with seriousness or are just words thrown out there, hoping you will accept them or even ignore them.

Active listening

There is a significant difference between hearing, listening and active listening.

- *Hearing* is a physical act where a person hears what is said, but

doesn't necessarily mentally process what is heard.
- *Listening* is a mental act where what is heard reaches that part of the brain that registers sound and interprets what is sent to it.
- *Active listening* is where a person is mentally engaged in the verbal exchange and makes connections based on circumstances, situations, relationships, expectations and understanding.

Everyone who doesn't have a hearing problem hears what another person says, but this doesn't mean they will act on it or even consider it.

Just being quiet while someone else is talking doesn't constitute real listening. Real listening is based on the intention of doing one of four things:

1. To understand someone
2. To enjoy someone
3. To learn something
4. To give solace or help

For example: While you are watching your favorite sport on TV, your spouse says, "Would you like something to drink?"

1. If you respond, "Sure, honey," without even considering what he or she has said, that's hearing, or passive listening.
2. If you were listening, you might respond, "Yes; what do we have?"
3. If you were actively listening you would respond, "Thanks, sweetheart, I'd like a can of beer."

The difference between these three examples is simply engagement.

When someone shares a fear or concern, or a need for validation, understanding or compassion, which of the three do you think would be the best approach?

Passive listening is simply fake listening masquerading as the real thing. The intent is not to listen, but to meet some other need such as

- Making people think you are interested so they will like you.
- Looking for one specific piece of information while ignoring everything else.
- Buying time so you can prepare for your response.
- Half listening so someone will listen to you.
- Looking for vulnerabilities so you can take advantage of them.

- Looking for the weaknesses in their argument or statement so you can take advantage of them.

So, what prevents people from active listening?

There are both internal and external factors.

Internal factors would be mental distractions, opinions, judgments, attitudes or beliefs. External would be a noisy environment, physical distance or any distraction that requires our attention, focus or concentration to overcome it.

It's easy to understand why so little, real, active listening takes place on a regular basis. In fact, research and studies have proven that most people spend less than 5% of their total communication time in active listening. So, is it any wonder why communication breaks down and commitments are easily made without real intent to follow-through?

There are many blocks to effective listening. Here are some of the common ones:

1. *Distractions:* such as a noisy environment
2. *Comparing:* a mental process of always comparing what you are hearing to whatever you have heard in the past that is in some way similar. This act tends to keep your mind in the past and not engaged in the present conversation.
3. *Mind reading:* trying to anticipate what the other person is saying as they are talking. This will tend to keep you in the future rather than in the present moment in this conversation.
4. *Rehearsing:* thinking in advance how you will react or respond to what you are hearing
5. *Filtering:* hearing only what you want to hear or what you agree with or are comfortable with
6. *Judging:* blending your opinions, values, experiences, expectations or beliefs into what you are hearing. If they don't match, you will filter out what isn't consistent with yours.
7. *Dreaming:* taking a person's message to a different level. You hear them, but you are more focused on what could be rather than what is.
8. *Advising:* being more focused on fixing, changing or criticizing what the other person is saying.

9. *Sparring:* simply wanting to disagree, disparage or condemn the other person's point of view or comments
10. *Being right:* needing your ego to defend itself and to be right, no matter what
11. *Patronizing:* agreeing for the sake of agreeing. You may not agree, but it's not worth your effort to engage in a more in-depth conversation at this time or with this person.
12. *Derailing:* disliking what you are hearing, so you attempt to change the subject

To improve your active listening, you can do any or all of the following:

1. *Paraphrasing:* restating in your own words what you have heard the other person say
2. *Questions:* asking something about what they have said. This sends the message you are listening and keeps you actively engaged.
3. *Feedback:* offering insights or comments from your perspective about what you have heard
4. *Clarifying:* similar to paraphrasing, except it can include questions
5. *Listen with empathy:* knowing that everyone is doing their best, given their ability to express themselves, to be clear, focused, accurate or compassionate. Empathy is simply the desire to know or understand, while sympathy is to feel sorry for someone or just patronize or agree with them even though you may not.
6. *Demonstrate positive nonverbal messages:* (see the next section)
7. *Listen with awareness:* looking for congruence while listening (again, congruence means 'similar to'). You are looking for consistency or disconnect in the person's message.
8. *Stay in the present:* keeping your mind out of the past (experience, baggage, feelings) or the future (expectations, needs or wants).
9. *Total listening:* maintaining eye contact, leaning forward as the other person talks, and controlling or moving away from distractions.

Non-verbal messages

We communicate on many levels, but there are two primary methods of sharing information with others. They are verbal communication and non-verbal communication. Verbal communication comes from a person's conscious mind, while non-verbal messages come from their unconscious mind. If there is inconsistency in either of these two messages—in other words, if you are getting clear non-verbal acceptance, but verbal resistance —go with the non-verbal signals.

Let's assume a spouse or significant other asks their partner what is wrong and they say, "Nothing".

The words are clear enough. *Nothing* means *nothing,* right? Well, maybe so and then again, maybe not. It depends on the emotional content behind the words that will determine its accuracy. It is difficult to describe the emotional impact of non-verbal messages with the written word, so let me give you another example.

There are people today telling others they love them, and they don't even know what the words "I love you" mean. I overheard two young teenagers (maybe 14 or 15) the other day telling each other, "Oh, I am so in love with you!" Puppy love? Infatuation? Maybe. Long-term commitment? I doubt it.

Occasionally, people seem to get broad-sided in relationships because they say things like, "I never knew that was important to you." Or, "I didn't know you were unhappy." Or, "I didn't realize you were so upset."

To see what is really going on with another person requires that you pay attention to the words and also look beneath the words to the emotional content driving the message.

What does this have to do with the integrity of a message and its ultimate meaning?

The word that I have used frequently is *congruence.* If the verbal message is in line with or similar to the non-verbal signals that accompany it or reinforce it, then you can be assured the message is accurate and true, regardless of whether you like it, agree with it or are comfortable with it.

For example, let's say you ask your spouse if they are happy in your relationship, and they say "Yes", but while doing so, they look away from you, tighten their facial expression or lean away from you. That's incongruence: There is inconsistency between what they feel and what they are saying. However, if when they answer, they make eye contact, smile and lean toward you, then you can know their words are true.

Let's say you ask a customer if they are satisfied with your service, and they say "Yes", but frown, fold their arms and tighten their posture as they respond. Guess what? They are not really satisfied. So, why would someone say they are happy or satisfied when they are not?

It could be for hundreds of reasons, such as: not wanting to hurt your feelings, having a hidden agenda, avoiding conflict or just wanting to hide the truth, for whatever reason.

The key is to pay attention to both the words that are used and the way they are said. You don't have to be an expert on non-verbal communication to see these inconsistencies; you need only to pay attention and observe.

Research has indicated that there are over 10,000 facial expressions. Add to this the factors of vocal tone, inflection, body position and gestures and, well, it's easy to see that accurately reading another person's message is almost impossible unless you are an expert in this subject.

How about making this even more complex by adding in the concept of spatial relationships or what are referred to as proxemic zones? This is the distance that separates you from the other person you are communicating with, and here things can get a bit confusing. There are four proxemic communication zones:

1. The intimate zone is within two feet of you.
2. The personal zone is within two to four feet.
3. The social zone is within four to twelve feet.
4. The public zone is beyond twelve feet.

You can't have an intimate conversation with your spouse when you are in the social zone and you should not have a public conversation with someone when they are in your intimate zone.

Keep in mind that these rules can change, depending on the culture. For example, some cultures feel that in a social conversation, you should be in someone's intimate zone, while other cultures would find this offensive.

Here are a few things you can do to improve your understanding of non-verbal communication, which will improve your listening and conversational skills:

1. Are the signals being sent by the other person open or closed

signals? Open signals are when a person moves closer to you, leans toward you, uncrosses their arms or legs, looks at you or makes eye contact. Closed signals are the opposite.

2. Notice if there is any increase or decrease of open or closed signals. This is another way to determine the integrity of their message.
3. Pay attention also to vocal tone, inflection and volume. If a person pauses a lot, hesitates, lowers or raises their voice or talks a lot faster or slower, these evidence possible incongruence or inconsistency in their words and message.

Generally, people don't automatically demonstrate all open or all closed signals in a conversation (as these are unconscious behaviors), while language is a conscious act. In other words, we choose our words, but the way we back them up or reinforce them is usually unconscious.

Let me repeat: If there is inconsistency between a person's verbal and non-verbal message, their non-verbal message will always be a more accurate expression of their thoughts, feelings or attitudes.

You are responsible to people, not for them

One of the concepts I share in my relationship programs is that we are responsible to people, but not for them.

We are responsible to our employees, friends, customers, children, spouse and anyone that crosses our path, but we are not responsible for their opinions, feelings, attitudes, life dramas, issues, problems and so on. It is the difference between detachment and disengagement:

- *Detachment* is when you own your emotional reactions or stuff: e.g., I will listen, care, be interested in, but not responsible for.
- *Disengagement* is when you don't give a rip about what the other person is experiencing.

Many people find that a lot of their relationship stress comes from taking responsibility FOR the other person's emotional stuff.

Your emotional reactions to anything and everything are yours and yours alone. You can attempt to draw me into your dramas, but it is up to me to decide whether I choose to detach or disengage (see above). Detachment is healthy, while disengagement contributes little if anything to healthy, loving, long-term relationship success.

You can see many instances of this condition in relationships, such as:

- Money stuff
- Career stuff
- Additive behavior stuff
- In-laws' stuff
- Children stuff
- Weight stuff
- Etc.

Therefore, I am not responsible for your use of words or the lack of consistency between your words and behavior. It is, therefore, up to me whether I allow you to 'set me up' with your words.

The use of 'don't'

Ever heard someone say to you, "Don't you think ...?" "Don't you feel ...?" "Don't you believe ...?" What's going on here?

When you say to someone, *don't you*, you are implying that they 'should'. "Don't you feel that people should return phone calls?" Again, you are implying that they should agree with your point of view. Instead, why not replace *don't you* with, *"Do you* think . . . , feel . . . or believe . . . ?" Or, "What do you think . . . , feel . . . or believe . . . ?" In other words, *ask* them what they think, feel or believe; don't tell them what they should feel, think or believe.

Vocabulary

I mentioned before that there are over 250,000 words in the dictionary. Is it possible, then, that when two people speak together, there is a real possibility that they may use a word or words that the other person is not familiar with or does not know its meaning? Yes, of course.

So, if a person admits they are not completely honest with their words or responses because they are diffident, and you don't know what *diffident* means and don't ask for clarification, then it's entirely possible that you could respond inappropriately to their message or statement. (By the way, *diffident* means *shy.)*

If a person uses a lot of slang or words that are colloquial or based on a part of the country or world where a word can have a totally different connotation or meaning, confusion is likely to ensue. For example, Southerners can often be heard to say, "That is sweet" or "You are sweet." Simple enough, right? Well, not entirely. Many Southerners may use that word in a condescending way. So, words are not always just words. (If you're from the South, please don't take offence, because I learned this from a Southerner.)

If a reliable business person says they will meet you for lunch at 12:30, and you are from a part of the world where 12:30 means 12:30(ish)—well, you can see how there might be some disconnect here.

The key when communicating is that if you are not sure of the other person's meaning or real intent, ASK.

Now that I have covered the basics, let's get into some practical applications of many of the ideas, techniques or concepts I have laid out for you in the previous sections.

The impact of the inconsistency of words

Human interactions are challenging at best, due to the variances of upbringing, education, experience and values, but add to this mix the complex concept of human communication and—well, when two people exchange feelings, ideas or experience through the use of words, anything is possible.

Each of us has a paradigm of how we feel we should be treated by others and how we will treat others.

In later sections, I'll discuss this concept as it applies to personal relationships and careers, but for now I'd just like to discuss the different ways in which our communication can lead to conflict, hurt feelings, disappointment and even anger.

At the risk of being redundant, let me review a few of the basics that I have covered:

1. Everyone has a unique perceptual filter that impacts their interpretation of the words and acts of others.
2. No one looks at life exactly the same.
3. Everyone has agendas, whether noble or otherwise.
4. Everyone wants to be treated with respect and compassion.
5. Words are more than just words and they can be interpreted or misinterpreted depending on a variety of other factors.
6. It is impossible to predict how another person will react or respond to our words, questions or conversations.
7. Real intent, rather than stated intent, is always more accurate when a person makes a promise or commitment.
8. A lack of clarity will always contribute to misunderstanding, confusion or conflict.
9. Making assumptions about what another person says or believes is a setup for disappointment and frustration.

When you consider the communication interactions between individuals, regardless of their circumstances or relationship type, it is important to understand that there are more than just words being exchanged when two or more people share feelings, attitudes, beliefs or opinions.

For example, things like:

1. The history of the relationship, whether new or long-term, will impact the interpretation.
2. The need, concern or desire for validation by anyone involved will drive how words are used, delivered and/or interpreted.
3. An individual's ability to handle conflict, confrontation, disagreement or misunderstanding will often determine how another's words are understood or handled.
4. A person's ego will often determine what words are used and why and how, as well as how words are interpreted.
5. Personal agendas or the need to manipulate others can drive conversations.
6. The lack of emotional control or maturity will influence the quality of conversation.

These are just some of the common elements that will impact any and all communication interchanges, often to the detriment of the quality of the overall relationship.

So, what exactly is inconsistency?

Primarily it's when something contradicts something else or that is not in keeping with it; in other words, it can be perceived as argumentative, filled with potential tension and often manipulative.

There can be a variety of results, mostly negative, when there is inconsistency between words, intent, how the words are delivered and perceived, how they are understood or processed and ultimate behavior. Here are just a few to consider:

I use the word *promise* when telling you I am going to do something. The verb *promise* can be a very misleading word, because its ultimate outcome may be determined by factors that you can't control.

- "I promise to play tennis with you this Saturday"—but it rains.
- "I promise to take you out to dinner tonight"—but the car breaks down.
- "I promise to get the report done by the end of the day"—but the

information I need to complete it is not available, due to a technical breakdown.

- "I promise to babysit for the kids this Saturday so you can have a play day with your friends"—but my boss says I have to work all weekend.

Then there words like, *I will always* and *I will never*.

1. "I will always treat you with respect"—but due to my stressors, I lose it.
2. "I will always put you first"—but you start taking me for granted, so I change my mind.
3. "I will always give you my best"—but for whatever reason, I don't.
4. "I will always respond to your business inquiries in less than 24 hours"—but due to a family issue, I have to be off work for a few days.
5. "I will never disappoint you." (Come on, get real here.)
6. "I will never leave you...." (Blah, blah, blah.)
7. "I wish you would always ___ (fill in the blank)."
8. "I want you to always ___ (fill in the blank)."
9. "I will never say 'whatever' again." (Sure!)
10. "I will never do [whatever] again." (Ditto)
11. "Why can't (won't) you ever . . . ?" (Come on now!)

See the problem here? We can always say these things, even with positive intent or integrity, but we can't always control the circumstances that may change or impact the outcomes.

So, what's the answer? Never promise? Never say, "I will never . . . "? Never say, "I will always . . . "?

As I've said earlier: The critical thing to observe when people use these types of words is to understand the difference between an occasional instance and a recurring pattern or trend in behavior.

If I say "I promise" a lot and seldom honor these statements, you can bet that every time I say it, I may be setting you up for disappointment or even worse. But if I say, "I will always" a lot, and in most situations I follow through, consistent with my words, then the chances of any setting up or disappointment will tend to be less.

If I say, "I will never hurt you emotionally or let you down"—but then out of the blue I do, there could be any number of reasons (such as fear, guilt, anger, resentment, stress or many other emotional contributors) that will impact the congruence between my words and actions. Not to mention, our relationship.

So, what's the outcome when words and results are inconsistent? Here are just a few:

- Loss of trust
- Disappointment
- Resentment
- Communication breakdowns
- Increased relationship stress
- Loss of respect
- Anger

To avoid these negative consequences, it is essential that you:

- actively listen,
- get clarity from the other person,
- pay attention to communication trends,
- ask more questions,
- consider the relationship history and its typical behaviors,
- clean out your mental filter,
- manage your expectations,
- and hold others accountable when they let you down because of their issues, and not because a situation isn't within their control.

The idea to keep in mind as we move forward into the final sections is this: When someone speaks, they can say what they really feel, think or believe—or what they say will advance their personal interests without regard for any degree of integrity at all.

In the end, this type of disconnect will cause you a great deal of inner turmoil.

Relationships and words

When two people are in a relationship, there will always be breakdowns in communication. This can result in conflict, disappointment and frustration if they allow these situations to have a negative impact on the quality of the relationship as a whole.

It's impossible for two people in a relationship not to eventually have a misunderstanding or a negative outcome because of miscommunication or making assumptions. This is normal and to be expected. But such instances do not have to negatively influence the respect, love and harmony that is present and hopefully growing.

The key is to develop methods or techniques for managing these potential relationship hazards.

When two people live under the same roof and have a history together, they tend to develop routines for dealing with their communication. These routines can be positive, negative or neutral in terms of their impact on the quality of the relationship.

Another factor that will always affect the quality of a couple's communication is how they handle intimacy, romance and love. At the expense of clarity, couples will often stuff feelings, attitudes and emotions, for any number of reasons.

For example: Some people use a variety of manipulative approaches when it comes to mutual relationship satisfaction.

It's common knowledge that some people are fond of using sex as a tool to get what they want, while others use guilt or emotional manipulation to get what they want or even coerce their partner into satisfying their needs or desires.

I'm certainly not suggesting that these approaches are positive or even beneficial when it comes to the overall health of a relationship, but many of these people are willing to sacrifice the overall relationship success to their short-term and often selfish motives. As I have stated throughout this book:

when someone speaks, they can say what they really feel, think, believe or what they believe will advance their personal interests without regard to any degree of integrity in their words at all.

When people in relationships say what they feel

Expressing true feelings is often difficult for many people, for a variety of reasons. Whether having low self-esteem, letting the ego override their emotions, needing to be liked, hoping to avoid conflict or needing to not hurt someone's feelings—any of these will cause someone to stuff their own feelings and often play the role of victim in their relationship.

It has been proven in the fields of medicine and psychology that holding back feelings or emotions will, over time, negatively impact a person's mental and physical well-being.

Saying what you really feel is an empowering way to live. It permits you to have integrity between what you feel, what you say and, ultimately, how you behave or what you do. This doesn't mean that you are right or that another person needs to honor or even care about your feelings; but it does allow you to avoid the inner stress of hiding behind the fears that prevent the expression of what is going on in your heart or mind.

If sharing your feelings is a positive approach to effective communication, why do so many people, especially men, avoid it?

Entire books have been written on this important topic, and it's not my intent to usurp or disagree with much of the literature that is available. I will simply say that this emotional avoidance is not just a male challenge and that developing the willingness, courage and skill to break through these barriers will, over time, free a person of the guilt, anger, frustration and the stress of keeping these feelings hidden behind a wall of insecurity.

When people in relationships say what they think

Everyone has varying degrees of knowledge, experience and opinions about a vast array of topics. Just because someone thinks something is right, good, best or true doesn't mean that it is for anyone or everyone else.

We all have opinions, whether religious, political, business or relationship. These opinions often become our 'shoulds' for those with whom we share our life. We defend our views, we argue our opinions and we try to influence or persuade others that our views are better or more right or appropriate then theirs.

Too often, people fail to say what they really think for any number of reasons, such as:

1. the fear of rejection,
2. the desire to be liked or accepted,
3. the attempt to avoid conflict,
4. the need to feel superior,
5. the desire to be always in control,
6. the need to not hurt others' feelings,
7. the need to protect their own experience,
8. the need to keep their ego intact,
9. and/or the need to demonstrate their knowledge, wisdom or mastery of some life area.

Saying what you think, without a manipulative agenda, is a healthy approach as long as you don't get too attached to the other's need to agree with you or to buy-in to your philosophy or version of truth.

Do you know someone who always tells you what they think? Do you know others who hold back, for one or more of the above reasons? Do you always say what you think—or do you hold back, protecting some personal agenda?

It takes courage, maturity, high self-esteem and self-acceptance to always share your thoughts with others and not betray your integrity due to circumstances or who is on the receiving end.

When people in relationships say what they believe

Beliefs are the result of emotional conditioning, most of which was accomplished before we hit the age of ten. We have been conditioned by parents, teachers, relatives, friends and religious leaders (among others too numerous to mention).

These people who influenced our beliefs along life's path were not right or wrong, but just shared with us what they learned and came to believe during their years of experience. They have, therefore, passed along to us their views, opinions, rights and wrongs that they refined during their learning and lifetime.

The problem for each of us arises when we unconditionally accept these views without question or challenge, and let this conditioning rule our future, personal growth, maturity, beliefs and ultimate interpretation of our own personal experiences.

If you are in a relationship with someone who can't handle your views or beliefs, and you decide the best way to have harmony in the relationship is to hold them back or even compromise them, doing so is a recipe for disaster at every level.

It takes courage and self-confidence to always say what you believe, regardless of who is on the receiving end of a particular conversation or what the circumstances are.

When people in relationships say what they believe to selfishly advance their own agendas

Relationships are not always easy. They require a variety of attitudes, skills and emotional maturity, as well as the willingness to compromise and be flexible, in order to ensure that any conflict due to breakdowns in communication are handled with compassion, respect and understanding.

Think for a moment about the last conflict you had in a relationship, and I'll guarantee that its cause was a disconnect between what was said, what was meant, how it was perceived and/or how all of these factors were handled or mishandled.

As I look back on many of my relationships and how and why they ultimately ended, I can tell you that in almost every case, it was due to a misunderstanding or conflict of some sort that wasn't handled well.

My former wife had agendas—and, yes, I had them, too; but over the long term, we failed to communicate with integrity and compromise. I'm not saying that all relationships have this negative practice or outcome, but I do believe that sooner or later, when communication isn't clear or congruent, everyone will have to deal with the emotions and negatives of either misunderstanding or confusion of what was said or done, or not said and not done.

As I have said, it's been proven that men's and women's brains are wired differently and as a result, both parties will often see any situation or circumstance differently. This is not to imply that either person is wrong, but that when a communication between a man and a woman takes place, the potential for misunderstanding is always lurking in the wings.

This is also not meant to imply that conversations between two men or two women will not face this same hazard. I'm only saying that the tendency for conflict is greater between two people of the opposite gender.

Think about three simple words spoken by a man or a woman, I *love you.* Do both parties mean the same thing when they utter these simple words?

Well, love and its expression and interpretation can vary greatly due to each person's understanding of it, but we also must consider if these words are spoken with an often subtle agenda or expectation.

How about when a man or a woman asks a simple question of their partner: "Are you happy or fulfilled in our relationship?"

Wow! Depending on any number of factors, this seemingly simple question can trigger all sorts of responses: some charged with the outcome of improving the relationship, while others could contribute to confusion, frustration or even resentment.

Add to this the fact that maybe there are underlying issues that are contributing to the person's answer, which may be grounded in fear, uncertainty or even manipulation.

Everyone has emotional, physical and psychological needs and wants. Some of these may be supplied by another person in a relationship; but sooner or later, if you are depending on your inner peace and happiness from another person, you will be disappointed.

I am by no means suggesting that people in a relationship shouldn't be there for their partner in a way that their partner needs. I am just saying that eventually everyone's happiness and inner peace is their own responsibility.

One's happiness, inner peace and contentment are not found in another person. Yes, others can contribute to its presence or the lack of it; but if these qualities are lacking in the relationship, you might want to first look in the mirror and not point your finger at your partner.

Integrity between communication and behavior will always be due to each person's ability to bring this attitude and congruence to the relationship. When both people bring them, a relationship can be filled with compassion, harmony, joy and ultimate long-term success.

When one or both people fail to bring this integrity to a relationship and blame any drama on their partner, this is a recipe for conflict.

There are a number of things you can do to improve the congruence between words and actions in a relationship. Here are three to consider:

1. Remember when you first fell in love? How you felt, what you were willing to accept and how you were willing to compromise and remain flexible, no matter what the behavior of your partner was? Bringing these mindsets back into the present, no matter how long you've been in the relationship, will go a long way in maintaining harmony, acceptance and understanding.
2. Remember your wedding vows? No matter whether they were traditional or you created them. Do you still honor them as the years pass? If not, what is getting in the way of maintaining these vows as you grow together?
3. Remember how you were tolerant of 'perceived' weaknesses, traits or idiosyncrasies in the other? How you didn't let trivia sabotage the present moments? The key to keeping conflict to a minimum in times of stress, disappointment and anxiety is to stay focused on your partner's good points, and not on what you perceive as those that are negative or need to change.

Keep in mind that all differences can be resolved as long as you are willing to have open, honest and nonjudgmental conversations around any topics that might be tension-filled.

One technique that can have a positive outcome on the communication style is to have a weekly 'conversation time' around those issues that cause you or your partner to withdraw, blame, defend yourself or just circle the wagons.

Let's wrap this section up with a simple clarification:

- What do men want to hear? Men want to hear words of validation, respect, encouragement and support.
- What do woman want to hear? Women want to hear feelings, compassion, understanding and reassurance.

When either persona hears such words, regardless of the speaker's intent or truth, they will tend for the short term to be appeased and feel important and valued.

The problem occurs when such words are not grounded in truth; sooner or later, the truth will emerge and when it does, the consequences could be even worse than having dealt with the truth earlier.

Careers and words

Words and actions can leave a lasting impact on a relationship. People will tend to remember for years the things you said and did, or the things you didn't say and didn't do. This is just as true for the negatives as it is the positives.

Does this mean we need to carefully edit each sentence, words spoken and action taken before we say or do something? Well, *yes* and *no* and *it depends*.

Whether it is a conversation with a customer, colleague or your boss, words can help your career or send it into a rapid slide to nowhere before you know it.

Whether in a meeting of your peers, a telephone conversation with a customer, an email to a supervisor or a text to your office mate, if these words can be misunderstood, they generally will be. In other words, if something can be misunderstood, it most likely already has been.

Words and a lack of congruence with a colleague—"Let's meet in the cafeteria for lunch at noon"—and you are late, won't necessarily put your career in jeopardy. But telling your boss, "I'll get this project completed by the end of the day"—and it doesn't happen ... well, any consequence is possible.

If you have ever purchased anything, I'll guarantee that as a consumer you have been told one thing by the vendor when you know that something else happened. Is this wrong? Incompetence? Misleading? Or just life happening? Could be all or any of these.

So, why do employees say things to their supervisors, customers or colleagues that eventually contribute to stress, uncertainty, fear or disappointment? And are some of these commitments, statements or promises designed to mislead or confuse others, or are people just interacting with other people in a normal, 'life happens' way?

Let me repeat: Clear and consistent communication is a challenge at best, and congruence between what people say and do will never be perfect or 100% accurate, for any number of reasons. But when it comes to your career or dealing with customers, employees or supervisors, many of these inconsistencies can contribute to poor customer loyalty, poor department effectiveness or even an unsuccessful career.

I have participated in numerous business meetings where people said things they didn't mean, for any number of reasons:

1. They agreed with management verbally and publically— when they believed otherwise.
2. They made promises to colleagues that a problem would be solved—and it wasn't.
3. They offered assistance or help with a project or activity—and they failed to follow through.
4. They set goals, made plans and committed to objectives—and these were not met or satisfied, for one reason or another.
5. They said whatever was expected, rather than what they really believed or felt.

Why?

Fear? Insecurity? Ego? Arrogance? Security? The avoidance of confrontation or conflict? Or just the desire to please, for the short term?

Yes, no, and again, *it depends!*

In my book *Corporate Disconnect* (Worldwide Press, 2009), I discuss many of the reasons for these types of breakdowns; let me share some of that information here.

Employee disconnect

1. When the realities that exist at the lower levels of an organization and in the market place do not find their way to the highest levels of the organization—where direction is set, goals are established, vision is created and major decisions are made—with accuracy, continuity, clarity and consistency.
2. When the vision, purpose, direction and leadership at the highest levels of an organization do not accurately radiate throughout the entire organization with integrity, accuracy, clarity, accountability and consistency.

3. When lack of corporate-wide congruence negatively impacts sales, profits, effectiveness and consistently healthy growth.

Presidents, CEO's, CFO's and other senior executives are typically flying at the 40,000-foot level in their organizations. They can see a long way. Their vision for the future is clear and they can easily be aware of major storms or opportunities at this altitude. But details? Not a clue. Middle managers, directors or senior staff employees are typically flying at the 20,000-foot level in their organizations. They don't have as clear a view of the horizon as their superiors, since they are 20,000 feet lower, but their view of the details is a bit more evident; not totally clear, but better than at the 40,000-foot level.

Then there are the employees in your organization who are flying at the 500-foot level, almost at ground level. They don't have a clue what's going on beyond their desk or the building next door, but they can tell you what customers think, what policies or procedures are working or not working and what is generally going on in the bowels of the organization. They know the details, they live them every day; but they, for the most part, don't always see the connection between the reality at 500 feet and the vision or decisions at 40,000 feet.

Here's the simple truth: If the reality of what is going on in the marketplace, with your customers, with your competitors and/or with your employees is not getting to the 40,000-foot level, I'll guarantee you are experiencing CD. Likewise, if the vision, leadership or goals at 40,000 feet are not finding their way to the 500-foot level, I'll guarantee you are also experiencing many of the negative issues of CD in your organization.

So, what is Corporate Disconnect? It's when your employees who do the work don't see a connection of their efforts to the vision of your senior management. It's when your senior management makes decisions or takes actions at the 40,000-foot level—new policies, new products or services, acquisitions, new divisions or branches, new anything—and they do it without getting in touch with the reality at 500 feet.

Beware! This is a recipe for lost customers, lost revenue, lost growth, poor employee retention, and any other negative corporate malaise imaginable.

One of the common errors poor managers make is to shoot the messenger who brings bad news. (Their subtle message is, "Don't bring me no bad news.") Their attitude towards the messenger is often:

1. You are not a team player.
2. You are always negative.
3. You are always complaining.
4. You are never happy.
5. You are a pain in the a_ _.

I'll agree that some employees fit one or all of the above characterizations. However, when you have an employee bring you bad news, do you:

1. Thank them?
2. Criticize them?
3. Ignore them?
4. Berate them?
5. Listen to them?
6. Encourage them to tell you more?
7. Other________________________________

The point is, the closer you are to reality (either with a situation inside the organization or outside with customers or suppliers), the better decisions you can make. This will contribute to the organization's performance and success. Shooting the messenger is a great way to ensure you stay totally out of touch with the conditions, perceptions, attitudes, problems and challenges that are present in your department or organization as a whole.

Mixed top-down messages

There is a great deal of confusion among employees in many of today's companies, due to the mixed signals that are being sent top-down in those organizations. Let me give you an example.

The president and executives spend three days hammering out a mission statement that will become the marching orders for the organization during the coming year. After careful wording, the group can finally agree on the scope, tone and meaning of the statement. It is presented to each employee in the form of a wall plaque that will be hung next to everyone's door, so it is the first thing they see every morning and the last thing they see each time they exit their office. The employees are required to memorize it and use it as their guide to decision-making and more productive behavior.

Let's say that one of the statements it contains is, "The customer always comes first in all of our dealings." A week after the statement has been presented to everyone; there is a dispute between two employees as to how to handle a customer complaint regarding the lack of warranty service. One says the customer didn't comply with the required paperwork, while the other states that even though the customer couldn't produce the required paperwork, the mission statement says the customer is to come first and that they should honor the complaint, regardless. The manager intervenes, and after learning the details of the issue, tells the employees that they cannot honor the warranty issue because the customer failed to produce evidence backing the complaint.

Both employees received the same mission statement. Unfortunately, the second employee's belief was verified that the mission statement was only words and should not be taken seriously in every situation. Although the manager agreed with the first employee regarding the outcome, the manager still interpreted the mission statement the same: empty words. These and thousands of similar examples can be found in every organization where inconsistent messages of any type are permitted, tolerated or even encouraged. Just imagine how confused the rank-and-file employee can become, wondering which message is accurate—depending on the weather, the time of the day, week of the month, month of the year, who is sending the message.

Another quick example that I am sure you can relate to if you have children, is the following. A daughter comes to her mother and asks if she can go out and play after dinner. The mom says *no, she has to get her homework done first.* The daughter doesn't like the answer, so decides to give it one more try. She asks dear old dad the same question, and he says, "Sure, honey, but make sure you come back in time to get your homework done." See the problem here? If you don't like the message from one person, find another. Trust me: This happens every day with working adults and not just ten year olds.

This confusion will ultimately lead to poor productivity, low morale, poor communication, poor customer relations, lagging sales and reduced margins and profits, as well as higher sales costs.

In a way, whenever there is a communication between two people, regardless of what kind of relationship, you can bet there is often a disconnect somewhere in the communication.

Political correctness and words

One of the issues that many people are concerned with when it comes to integrity-based communication is political correctness.

Definition: *relating to or supporting the use of language or conduct that deliberately avoids giving offense, e.g. on the basis of ethnic origin or sexual orientation.* I would add that we could include dozens more examples to this definition, given current political, social and other trends that are having tremendous influence on what we can say and who we can say it to while trying to avoid offending literally everyone.

Think about it for a minute: Even comedians can no longer pick on gays, obese people, Catholics, Jews, African Americans, Yankees, Southerners, illegal immigrants, the elderly, Democrats, Republicans, etc., etc., etc., without putting their career in jeopardy.

As a writer, I have a choice: say what I feel and believe—which doesn't mean it is right or wrong, good or bad, or relevant or not; it's just me expressing myself without degrading others—or edit every word or paragraph to ensure I don't upset you.

I will guarantee that no matter what you read or hear, sooner or later you can, if you choose, take what another person says personally—even if they didn't mean you specifically.

It comes back to intent. As Mark Twain once said, "If there is no malice in your heart, there can't be any malice in your words."

Yes, there are many nasty, prejudiced, opinionated and judgmental people in the world, but the question remains: If I can't say what I feel or believe without offending others, sooner or later I will just stop talking.

I don't mean to imply that we should not be sensitive to the lives and circumstances of others, but come on: If someone has to think about everything they say before they say it—well, you are only getting artificial words and feelings that may not be in any way accurate.

I recently heard that we need to stop calling people 'illegal immigrants' so we don't offend them. But that's what they've done, come into the U.S. illegally. So, what do we call them? *Unwanted guests? People who want a better life? International wanderers?*

What about obese people (no disrespect to them, whether or not they have medical conditions that contribute to their weight)? Do we call them *unfortunate overeaters? Sugar lovers? Nice big people?*

Or what about old people? *Friendly codgers? People who have been here a long time? Older young people?*

I could go on with these silly examples, but 1) I have offended you, 2) you are laughing or 3) you could care less and have skipped this section.

Sooner or later we will all be offended by the words of others. Get over it and just choose not to take these comments or words personally. It's called *maturity* and *growing up,* folks.

Having been in front of over a million people during my career as a speaker, I am confident there have been hundreds who didn't like what I said or how I said it. Again, get over it. There was no evil intent; just me being me.

I have been the greeter at the early service in my church for several years. The average person who attends this service is in their mid-80's. Each morning my goal is to make everyone feel welcome and yes, laugh. I'll bet there have been a few newcomers who on their first visit couldn't believe what they heard come out of my mouth. Let me default back to my mentor, Mr. Twain: There is no malice in my heart—ever.

One of my best friends is black. Oops, not politically correct. Gotta say, *African-American.* For us, it's not about skin color or ethnic origin, but the ability to let each of us be who we are in our relationship together. But I'll guarantee there are others, both black and white people, who shake their heads when they hear us talk together in what they would consider insensitive or even racist language.

For us, it's about being true to who we are and not editing our conversations through a race filter. We respect each other, and it has nothing to do with skin color.

I moved to the South over twenty years ago, and as a Yankee I have to tell you: There are some folks I've met here who view me strictly as a Yankee first and a person second. And, yes, there are many Yankees who have a similarly-jaundiced view of Southerners.

Come on. Do we have to be labeled by where we are from or how we talk? When I call some of my good Southern friends a *redneck* or *hick*, they don't get offended, because they know I am being playful, not rude. Of course I would not call a new Southern acquaintance one of these nicknames, as that would be an insult until we would get to know each other and accept this informality. This is called discretion, but I would add that discretion is a form of political correctness. So, learning to speak honestly must be blended with respect and compassion. But, in my opinion, it should never get in the way of personal self-honesty and expressing one's feelings, views or opinions.

Everyone filters what they see and hear through a very personal filter, and far too many people let this filter get in the way of potential relationships because of their prejudices or personal judgments.

You can agree or disagree with this whole issue of political correctness, but I have to tell you: If we keep increasingly worrying about offending anyone or everyone with what we say, sooner or later we will start offending dolphins, cats, ants and birds. Sound ridiculous? Well, just listen to or observe how the media, government and various organizations are trying to force us to speak only in certain ways when it comes to other groups, individuals, situations or life in general.

Inner peace and happiness, and words

We all want and many of us need validation, respect and encouragement. Each of us wants to feel valued and important. The problem surfaces when someone uses words to give us this temporary inner satisfaction, but they are just words and not based on the speaker's real attitudes about us.

This can be called, simply, an emotional set-up. We will feel a sense of inner peace or happiness hearing what we want, but this may dissipate when some other display of emotions or words from the other person contrasts to what we are trying to achieve internally.

Inner peace is not found in the words of others. It is not developed as a result of external circumstances such as fame, wealth, power, position or security. Inner peace is an acceptance that all is well, regardless of what is going on around you that may appear to be negative or challenging; and that you can handle it, overcome it, deal with it or even just survive with your contentment intact.

People who look to others or circumstances to provide inner peace will always be disappointed and often will feel betrayed.

One of the critical elements when it comes to inner peace and happiness is self-talk: the words, whether positive or negative, that keep floating through your mind.

I'm not talking here about just worry, fears or needs, but also the relentless replaying of old hurts, resentments, regrets and unmet expectations from others as well as yourself.

It's been said by many mental health professionals that most, if not all, of your inner soundtrack is nothing more than the replaying of the same inner thoughts over and over again.

It is difficult to find inner peace and happiness if your mental focus and thoughts are consistently negative, invalidating, pessimistic or self-depreciating.

It takes courage, practice, repetition and focus to keep your mind on what is good and beneficial in your life, and not bad for your inner calm and peace.

Here's how the mind works.

Although everyone's brain is made up of similar anatomy and billions of cells, research over the years has indicted that there are literally trillions of neural connections that have recorded every memory, experience, thought, action and behavior during a person's life. Everything a person has learned and their reaction to that learning is stored somewhere in that person's mind.

Evidence has also shown that due to the repetitive nature of neural function, over time people begin to think in similar ways and have predictable reactions to similar events, people and circumstances.

For example: A person who tends to be optimistic seems to have neural pathways in the brain that cause them to continue to act and think in positive ways, no matter what is happening in their life. And the brains of negative or pessimistic people have also created similar pathways that cause them to react in negative ways.

Think for a moment about the Grand Canyon. This Wonder of the World wasn't created because a river flowed through it for a few weeks and, therefore, we now have this incredible masterpiece of nature. In reality, it took millions of years for the flow of water to wear away at the rock and create the deep gorges that are now reality.

A person's brain seems to function in similar ways.

Think of 'the gorges' as grooves in the mind that have been created over time and with repeated similar thoughts, by the electrical synapses or brain connections moving electrical messages from one brain cell to another. It is easier for these impulses to travel the routes that have been previously carved out than to travel in new directions.

Generally speaking, a person who repeatedly tends to think positive thoughts has created pathways in the brain that the brain recognizes as the most comfortable route for these neural transmissions or thought patterns for this individual. This is why it is so hard for a positive person to be negative and vice versa.

For example: You hear a phrase that you neither agree nor disagree with, such as when someone says to you, "You just don't understand this concept;

it's obviously too complicated for you." The seed has been planted. Every time you are exposed to something complicated, your brain retrieves this little bit of information and reacts accordingly, bringing the thought back into your consciousness. The more this happens, the easier it is for your brain to retrieve this same thought pattern; thus the constant reminder that you just 'don't get it.'

Try observing your thoughts for the next five minutes, and I'll guarantee that most of them have to do with either past or future experiences, emotions, fears, hopes, worries or dreams. For most people, very few thoughts are 'present focused.' Why is this? It's simple: The unconscious doesn't like a vacuum or emptiness, so it will fill your conscious thoughts with *something,* whether you want it or choose it or not. Just try quieting your mind for five minutes and you'll understand. As you try to quiet your mind, thoughts, one by one, will fill your consciousness, whether you want them or not.

There is a second consideration and this has to do with a simple part of the brain called the medulla.

The medulla is the lower half of the brain stem and it functions primarily as a traffic cop.

As a person is exposed to new ideas, learning, concepts, people or experiences, these must first pass through the medulla before they can be moved into the conscious or unconscious mind. This region has no agendas, prejudices, hopes, dreams or opinions. It decides second-by-second about everything it is exposed to: *Does this idea or experience, etc., belong in the person's unconscious or conscious mind? Does the person need access to this information now or in the future?* If its conclusion, based on previous thought patterns, is that you don't need access to this information, now it will send the information straight to the unconscious for storage.

Think of the medulla as the on/off button on a computer, where the new program you want to install on your computer is housed. If the power is on and operating properly, the information is transferred to your hard drive, and may be made available on your RAM if you have given it these instructions. If the power is off and you are downloading information from the Internet while you are sleeping, the information is automatically moved to your hard drive, without your interaction or involvement. But if tomorrow morning you want access to it, all you have to do is turn your computer on—

and there it is.

Here's part of the problem when it comes to changing your thoughts. Most people go through their days in autopilot; in other words, they are not consciously aware, and they have turned over their reactions, responses and behaviors to automatic. They have given control of their behaviors, thoughts and actions over to their unconscious minds. Very few people live their lives 24/7 with conscious awareness or with what is called a 'presence consciousness': being in the now or the present moment. As a result, over 90% of the information, events, and experiences people are exposed to minute by minute, are routed by the medulla right into the unconscious mind.

The information is there and available for use, but the problem remains that if we are not consciously aware of what information has been stored, then how can we use it? It would be like the Internet downloading a software program onto your hard drive while you are at lunch; but when the download was complete, it never put an icon on your desktop or even listed it in your list of available programs. Yes, the information is there and can be used, but if you don't know it is there, you will never try to use the software for the purpose for which it was designed. So, it sits there in potential, waiting to be used, but never is.

Let's look at an everyday example of how a person has turned the control of their life over to their unconscious mind.

In the area of communication, research has indicated that the accuracy of a person's communication or messages is less than 10% verbal and around 25% tonal and over 50% nonverbal. You see, verbal communication, what you say, is generally a conscious act. You choose to say *yes* or *no* as a response to some request. However, the degree of honesty in your answer will be revealed over 75% by the way you deliver that *yes* or *no*. Verbal communication is a conscious act; and at the same time, nonverbal signals and messages such as gestures, body position, posture, inflection, vocal pace or volume, etc., will more accurately reflect whether the person really means *yes* or *no*.

Intention or *intent* means showing great determination to do something, something planned, or the purpose that accompanies a plan. It is a plan, goal, target or purposeful action. Intent is when a person really plans to do whatever necessary to honor their words, objectives, goals or plans.

So, when a person says they will give you a call and doesn't, what was their intent? There could be a number of answers:

- They never meant to call you, but didn't want to admit this at the time.
- They intended to call you, but something got in the way. (Refer to the earlier section where we discussed whether this is a simple instance or, if repeated, a habit or trend.)

One of the significant problems in human relations is that most people tend to pay more attention to another person's stated intent, assuming that they mean what they say, rather than trying to discover their real intent. I call this scenario the set-up! These people then act disappointed or surprised when the other person doesn't deliver or do what they said they were going to.

A person can consciously redo or reprogram their mental grooves (see above), but it takes time, patience, commitment, discipline, focus and the will to change. A lot of work? Yes. This is why so few people are able to reprogram their mental pathways to achieve the mental states they desire, thereby taking conscious control of the operation of their minds, feelings, emotions and behaviors.

People can change, but they have to want to change and they have to ensure that their stated intent is stronger than their unconscious, opposing intent.

If you want inner peace and happiness, you have to do two things:

1. Control what your mind is exposed to, and
2. learn to control the thoughts that you keep playing over and over again in your mind.

Summary

Words are just words. Not really. Words are the way humans share their feelings, knowledge, opinions, prejudices, fears, dreams and experiences with others, whether loved ones or total strangers.

Words can have any number of meanings or interpretations, depending on a person's mood, education, stress level, agendas, needs, desires or the history of a relationship.

When a person says something to you, you do more than hear their words; you filter them through a very personal mental set of expectations, guidelines, experiences and past thoughts.

Is it any wonder that there is so much disappointment, conflict, anxiety, misunderstanding and assumptions made when humans communicate?

In this book, I have shared a number of ideas, insights, opinions and attitudes about words, communication and behavior. As you have read, you too have filtered these words and interpreted them, agreed with them or disagreed with them—not because of the words that were on the pages, but because you brought any number of issues, mindsets, feelings or attitudes to the reading process.

You may have reacted one way to a concept or idea, while another person may have responded totally differently or even the opposite to you.

This is normal and to be expected. Given this simple idea, is it any wonder why people disagree, protect their beliefs, defend their views and often defensively dig in their heels when someone shares their views or attitudes about anything?

What's the answer to improved human understanding of words, intent, motives, behavior and the outcomes of all of these interactions?

It's simple and it's complicated.

Simple—if we would look past the words to try and discover a person's real Intent. Complicated—because this is often difficult, given our attachment to our experiences, expectations and the need to be understood, agreed with or accepted.

Caution: Words are just words, but their meaning and their ultimate outcome will impact the quality of every relationship, either negatively or positively. This book has been written to help promote more positive communication.

Define the following words

As I have said, words are more than their meaning, and their meaning can vary depending on how the word is used. I have given you numerous examples in previous chapters, but how about taking some time to define what the following words mean to you? If you are in a relationships with someone, how about asking them to define these words as well? I guarantee it will provide material for an interesting dialog. Have fun with this!

Agreeable

Aggressive

Aloof

Always

Apologize

Argue

Arrogant

Assertive

Bad

Badger

Baggage

Beliefs

Belligerent

Belittle

Blissful

Bossy

Caring

Carp

Censure

Challenge

Cherish

Cold

Commitment

Communicate

Compassionate

Complain

Compromise

Condescending

Congruent

Considerate

Contented

Correct

Criticize

Demean

Difficult

Disagree

Disparage

Distant

Dream

Dysfunctional

Ego

Emotions

Empower

Enjoyable

Expectations

Faults

Fear

Feelings

Feisty

Flawed

Flexible

Forever

Forgive

Friendly

Gentle

Good

Gracious

Grovel

Happy

Harass

Heartfelt

Help

Hidden agendas

Honesty

Hope

Ignore

Immature

Innuendo

Insecure

Interrupt

Invalidate

Judgmental

Judgments

Later

Lazy

Libido

Listen

Loving

Mature

Mindset

Nasty

Never

Nice

Nitpick

Now

Nurture

Obedient

Opinionated

Ornery

Paradigms

Patronizing

Perceptions

Perfect

Persuade

Pleasant

Promise

Punish

Pushy

Prejudices

Respect

Right

Sarcastic

Satisfied

Self-esteem

Selfish

Selfless

Sensitive

Settle

Share

Sincere

Someday

Stress

Stressful

Stubborn

Support

Tender

Thoughtful

Understand

Values

Vindictive

Whine

Withdrawn

Wrong

Recommended Reading

Acres of Diamonds, Conwell

An Enemy Called Average, Mason

Brain Rules, Medina

Celebrate Yourself, Briggs

Emotions of Normal People, Marston

Five Important Things, Paluch

Fully Human, Fully Alive, Powell

Getting the Love You Want, Hendrix

Halftime, Buford

Healing Words, Dossey

Handbook to Higher Consciousness, Keyes

How to Have Confidence and Power in Dealing with People, Giblin

In The Flow of Life, Butterworth

Jonathan Livingston Seagull, Bach

Life is Tremendous, Jones

Living the Simple Life, St. James

Love Busters, Harley

Man's Search for Meaning, Frankl

No Excuse!, Rifenbary

Personal Magnetism, DuBrin

Personality Plus, Littauer

The Seat of the Soul, Zukov

Self-Love, Schuller and Peale

Setting Your Heart on Fire, Cushnir

That's Life, Connor

That's Not What I Meant, Tannen

The Art of Loving, Fromm

The Bible

The Book of Secrets, Chopra

The Secrets Men Keep, Arterburn

The Bridge Across Forever: A Love Story, Bach

The Choice, Mandino

The Five Temptations of a CEO, Lencioni

The Greatest Miracle in the World, Mandino

The Language of Love, Smalley and Trent

The Mastery of Love, Ruiz

The Power of Positive Thinking, Peale

The Power of Patience, Ryan

The Psychology of Winning, Waitley

The Power of Intention, Dyer

The Road to Happiness is Full of Potholes, Connor

The Road to Happiness is Full of Potholes FunBook, Connor

The Trade-Off, Connor

The Transparent Self, Jourard

The Prophet, Gibran

The Voice of Knowledge, Ruiz

The Voyage, Connor

Transitions, Bridges

Try Giving Yourself Away, Dunn

Unconditional Love, Powell

Wakeup Calls, Allenbaugh

What Happy People Know, Baker and Stauth

What Could He Be Thinking?, Gurian

What a Man Wants, What a Woman Needs, Long

Wherever You Go, There You Are, Kabat-Zinn

When Everything Changes, Change Everything, Walsch

Why Am I Afraid to Tell You Who I Am?, Powell

Why Are We Here?, Connor

About the Author

Tim Connor, CSP

Tim is the bestselling author of over 80 books, including several international bestsellers. Titles include: *Soft Sell, 81 Challenges Smart Manages Face, Your First Year in Sales, 91 Mistakes Smart Salespeople Make, Corporate Disconnect* and *Overcoming Life's Challenges and Difficult Times.*

Since 1973 he has given over 4000 presentations in 23 countries to a wide variety of audiences.

Tim has been a member of the National Speakers Association for over 30 years and he is one of only 500 Certified Speaking Professionals in the world, a designation given by the National Speakers Association since 1973.

To order any of Tim's best selling books, CD's or other personal, career and business development learning materials please visit his website:

www.timconnor.com

Call his office at: 704-895-1230

Email him at: tim@timconnor.com